Rainmakers, Closers, and Other Sales Myths

Arnold Tilden

UNIVERSITY PRESS OF AMERICA,® INC.

Lanham • Boulder • New York • Toronto • Plymouth, UK

Copyright © 2007 by
University Press of America,® Inc.
4501 Forbes Boulevard
Suite 200
Lanham, Maryland 20706
UPA Acquisitions Department (301) 459-3366

Estover Road
Plymouth PL6 7PY
United Kingdom

Library of Congress Control Number: 2006930309
ISBN-13 978-0-7618-3548-6 (paperback : alk. paper)
ISBN-10 0-7618-3548-2 (paperback : alk. paper)

Contents

Foreword

I LOVE THIS BOOK!

That's the first thing I said to Arnie (aka Dr. Arnold Tilden) after I read *Rainmakers, Closers & Other Sales Myths*. As the saying goes, Arnie and I go way back. We have known one another for nearly twenty years and occasionally we have collaborated on projects through our respective consulting practices. He had asked me to look at *Rainmakers* in search of a pre-publication promotional quote. What he got instead is this foreword and my assertion that this will be one of the best books you will ever read on sales and sales leadership, two topics not only near and dear to my heart, but some of the core competencies of The Wiley Group. In other words, having worked with firms like The Ford Motor Company, Pfizer, Kellogg, Caterpillar, ExxonMobil, Gannett and Verizon to improve sales and in creating a Gettysburg based leadership experience, I know something about the content area of *Rainmakers*.

Rainmakers begins with the intriguing proposition that companies, even the biggest and brightest in their industries, subscribe to mythology when it comes to growing their businesses through selling. Like ancient societies, if it is something vitally important *and* modern businesses don't understand it, they turn to a myth. Except today's Rainmaker doesn't dance with a snake. Rather he performs his machinations with a laptop armed with the ubiquitous and mind numbing PowerPoint presentation while detached from the company's strategy.

Arnie's treatment of the four prevailing sales myths (Rainmakers, Closers, Schmooze and Field of Dreams) just rings so true to me. I have seen many companies fail to improve sales performance because of their blind pursuit of one or more of the myths Arnie outlines in the opening section.

Don't worry if you discover that your sub optimal sales performance is attributable to one or more of the sales myths. Dr. Tilden offers a prescription in a system that integrates *Strategy, Structure* and *People.* As he writes, all three need to be addressed and coordinated. It is not unusual for me to find organizations investing millions in training their people who never get the return they expect, because they are operating in an antiquated structure that measures the wrong things or rewards the wrong behaviors. I found the chapter on *Informal Structure* laugh out loud funny. This is where Arnie illustrates totally dysfunctional and reason defying sales structures that are held together by dotted lines connecting one job title to the next. What is not funny, is that I often see these very same organizational structures in real life, ones where it is impossible to determine who reports to whom.

Those of you familiar with my background know that I went to Gettysburg College, married the president's daughter (what better way to get through the academic rigor of that fine little college) and still today reside in the Gettysburg region. You may have also heard of our powerful *A Transformational Journey from Gettysburg* leadership program where we analyze and apply the leadership decisions that shaped our country's future at that famous Civil War battle (stevenbwiley.com).

Needless to say, I am a student of history and military strategy and a practitioner in how learning from it can transform modern day business leaders. While Arnie draws upon Sun Tzu's classic *Art of War,* from another era and another continent, I found his analogy between winning business and waging war utterly compelling. It is absolutely true that a winning business has to translate its strategy from the board room through the CEO's office right down to the trenches where sales managers and their teams of sales people are conducting hand-to-hand combat with the enemy. Do your sales people know the corporate strategy? Do your executives receive and analyze the reconnaissance your sales people deal with every day in the field? Try Arnie's simple test: ask them.

If you periodically look at the ads firms run for sales positions, as I do, you know that many list previous industry selling experience as a requirement. Dr. Tilden sheds light on this prevalent hiring mistake when he treats the third leg of the integrated sales success system: *People.* He cites the voluminous research done by the Gallup Organization (reported by Buckingham and Coffman (1999) in *First Break All the Rules)* which reveals that the best managers *don't emphasize experience* when recruiting. Instead, they focus on talent which Arnie defines as being natural and god given. The mantra Arnie puts forward is one that is often violated but essential to becoming a high performing sales organization. Repeat after me: *Recruit for talent. Train for skills.*

This isn't a text that you passively read while privately wondering what it has to do with you or your company's sales performance. Instead, the reader is challenged to complete a *Scorecard* at the conclusion of each chapter. Tell-tale symptoms for each of the sales myths are listed at the conclusion of the opening chapters to help you determine if you are in the grip of the *Rainmaker, Closers, Schmooze or the Field of Dreams* myths. The subsequent sections, detailing the *Strategy, Structure and People* system, each have a Scorecard as well. The valedictory chapter, Plan of Action, summarizes each of the scorecards and culminates in action steps to improve sales performance. There is no getting around concrete and practical steps for which the return on investment is unimaginable.

Here's what else I said to Arnie when I called him after reading *Rainmakers, Closers and Other Sales Myths*:

I couldn't put it down.

I love the way it balances great content with entertaining stories.

It is just great stuff!

I know you will come away with similar sentiments when you begin to turn the pages that follow. Please enjoy it as I did. Do the scorecard exercises and complete the plan of action in the concluding chapter and I am certain you will see tangible and measurable improvement in sales performance whether, it is for you individually, or for the team or organization you lead. I guarantee it!

Steven B. Wiley

Acknowledgements

I learned many of the concepts in this book from my partner in PfP Consulting, Inc., Harry Koolen. Our friendship stretches back to our days as classmates and fraternity brothers at St. Lawrence University.

Other friends reviewed drafts and offered both constructive criticism and encouragement. Among them are Roger Graham, retired from United States Department of the Treasury; Robert Wesoloskie, adjunct professor of business at Elizabethtown College; and Matthijs Van der Want, in Brussels, Belgium. Kimbra Shoop did the final copy editing and offered invaluable assistance.

Finally, I wish to acknowledge the distinctive contributions of my two daughters who, in addition to managing their careers and my grandchildren, found time to help. Kelly reviewed all of the contracts and legal documents that accompany a project like this, and Rachael had the patience to read and critique the very first draft. To all of you, a very sincere "Thank you".

How to Use This Book: Scorecards

To get the most from this book it should be read actively, evaluating your own approach to selling or sales management along the way. To guide that process, *Scorecards* are listed at the conclusion of most chapters (one, fourteen and seventeen are the exceptions). As the term suggests, they should help you *score* yourself, or your organization, on the contents of that chapter.

The Scorecards in Section One (Debunking the Mythology of Selling) challenge you to consider your susceptibility to the prevailing sales myths: Rainmakers, Closers, Schmooze and Field of Dreams. Those in Section Two through Four invite the reader to consider, respectively, the effectiveness of their *Strategy, Structure* and *People*.

All of the Scorecards are compiled in the concluding chapter: Plan of Action. Employing Peter Drucker's terminology (2005), chapters one through sixteen help the reader identify what the *right things are* to improve sales performance. Chapter Seventeen, on the other hand, is a guide for the reader to develop and implement a plan to get the *rights things done*.

DEBUNKING THE MYTHOLOGY OF SELLING

"Put that coffee down! Coffee is for closers!"

Blake (Alec Baldwin) to Shelly (Jack Lemon)
In Glengarry GlenRoss

Chapter One

Mythology & Selling

Every business shares a similar storyline, from corporate giants like Microsoft to Two Bobs with a Truck.

FOUR STEPS TO BUSINESS EVOLUTION

Step One: A Unique Value Proposition

The initial step is to determine a unique value proposition: the software that has transformed Microsoft into a $34 billion a year powerhouse to chimney cleaning by two guys named Bob who wear top hats.

Regardless of how seemingly common on the surface, every enterprise claims to have or do something that distinguishes it from the competition. Look closely enough and you will find the proclamation of being the bigger, better, cheaper, smarter, smaller, faster, only, distinctively attired, oldest, closest, newest, friendliest, most caring business in the field, industry, region, or world.

Barclays Global Investors is the world's biggest manager of retirement assets. Geisinger Health Plan is the largest rural provider of health coverage. Johnson Controls delivers best in class integrated building systems. Susquehanna University is number one among regional liberal arts colleges in the northeast. KPMG is nationally recognized as the leading senior living care consulting firm. Southwest Airlines offers cheaper airfares. McDonald's is the fastest restaurant. Lexus is more than a car. It's a whole new category. Glenlivet was the first single malt scotch to arrive in America. Goodyear is number one in tires. Using different measures, Harvard, Penn, and William and Mary all claim to be the oldest institution of higher learning in the United

States. Hooters features distinctively attired wait staff. And everybody knows your name at Cheers.

At least the founders of the enterprise, and the others close enough to be involved in the planning process, (regardless of how formal it is) know and believe in the unique value proposition. Sometimes they even believe it with a passion.

Step Two: Infrastructure

When the business founders are right about the distinctiveness of their value proposition, their businesses begin to grow. Early success in sales prompts two internal steps. Enterprises move to make certain that orders are filled or services delivered in a fashion that customers or clients have come to expect. In manufacturing, this often takes the form of commitment to principles of quality assurance. Microsoft can't withstand software that crashes (too often, anyhow) and the two Bobs can't send a third guy out to clean chimneys in a baseball cap instead of a top hat. Step two is putting an infrastructure in place to ensure that consumers of the product or service are getting the unique value they bought.

Step Three: Internal Business Processes

Once quality issues are addressed, organizations put internal processes in place, often to satisfy industry or government regulations. Chief financial officers pop up sporting titles like controller, comptroller, business manager, or vice president. Then human resource professionals are brought on to ensure adequate diversity in hiring, that promotions and firings are on the up-and-up, and hostile environments aren't brewing along with the coffee.

To recap, the business story progresses like this: Step one is to develop, invent, think-up, inherit, steal, or buy a product or service with a unique value proposition. Step two is to ensure quality is not compromised once the enterprise starts to grow and personnel other than the founders are relied upon to deliver the product. Step three is to add staff to manage internal processes like financial affairs and human resources.

Step Four: Subscribe to One or More Sales Myths

Step four, sustaining growth by adding a sales function, is where things get wild and weird. Here, rather than following a course guided by logic and reason, businesses behave like the ancient Greeks and resort to mythology.

SIMILARITIES BETWEEN MYTHS AND SELLING

Throughout history there have been intellectual wars waged by forces subscribing to *myths* and rationalists pursuing a course guided by *logic*. It's appropriate to note that both words are, in fact, derived from Greek: myth from *mythos* and logic from *logos*.

Most businesses rely on mythology because they don't understand the selling process, pursing instead modern sales myths, such as *Rainmakers, Closers, Schmooze and Field of Dreams*. We systematically debunk each of these modern myths in the chapters that follow.

First, however, let's identify some similarities between the cultures that pursued myths and the modern business organizations that still do.

There are eight similarities between mythology and selling.

1. Stories about heroic exploits get retold
2. The underlying truth of the myths gets taken for granted
3. Different cultures subscribe to different myths
4. Poets spread the word
5. Priests and consultants interpret the word
6. They both celebrate hunting
7. Live sacrifices are made to appease those who can make it rain
8. There's a little bit of truth in the myths

Stories about Heroes

Myths are basically stories that have been retold to help a culture make sense of processes too difficult for mere humans to understand. Although mythology was at the core of their culture, the ancient Greeks were not alone in their beliefs. Scandinavians had Thor, Romans followed Odysseus, the Old Testament tells the story of Moses, Cuchulain was a great Irish warrior, and Americans spread tales of Paul Bunyan (Wilkinson 1998).

All of these figures demonstrated great character and heroism in winning battles over feared adversaries. The more their stories were retold, the bigger the heroes became (in Paul Bunyan's instance, literally). And with each retelling, the more accepted the techniques became.

In selling, representatives who are mere mortals are sent out to do battle with sales prospects, the modern sales hero's adversary. They encounter many challenges during their adventures — from gatekeepers throwing up obstacles, to competitors cutting prices, to disinterested buyers who object to every conceivable benefit.

Truths Gets Taken for Granted

When they return home victorious with a sale, today's sales heroes gather the other warriors around the modern day campfire and, fortified by a few beers, recount the tale of the battle. As with the ancient heroes who preceded them, modern selling stars emphasize the character and courage they demonstrated on the hunt. Yes, it took tenacity to handle those rejections. Great cunning was executed in handling the objection. But, ultimately, it was courage and testosterone that closed the sale.

Eventually, sales heroes and their disciples believe without question that techniques like closing and handling objections are the keys to winning sales battles. In truth, however, reason supported by research would show that nothing is further from the truth.

Different Cultures—Different Myths

There are other similarities between selling and mythology. Each city in ancient Greece devoted itself to one or more, but not all, of the gods on Mount Olympus. Similarly, businesses usually subscribe to one or two, but not all, of the sales myths. A professional practice believing in Rainmakers may also Schmooze its clients, but not subscribe to the Field of Dreams or Closers myths. Conversely, a manufacturing firm founded and led by engineers may subscribe exclusively to the Field of Dreams myth and battle internally for more research and development dollars rather than wasting valuable resources on Schmooze.

Poets Spread the Word

Ancient cultures learned about the feats of their mythological heroes, not only through word of mouth, but also from poets. Those writers of unsubstantiated opinion promoting techniques like closing or handling objections are today's sales poets. They attract thousands of followers to their rallies where hungry disciples stand in long lines to buy their books and tapes loaded with empty pabulum. Sales managers believing those myths spread the word when they recruit talent with advertisements like, *Only closers need to apply.*

Priests Interpret the Word

Priests with no special powers interpreted the words of the gods for the ancient Greeks. Today that role is played by consultants who interpret gods like Collins (*Good to Great*), Kaplan & Norton (*The Balanced Scorecard*), Covey (*Habits of Highly Effective People*), Lencioni (*Five Dysfunctions of a Team*) and Buckingham (*First Break All the Rules* and *The One Thing You Should Know*).

No matter how powerful the god, merely listening to a priest, or a consultant for that matter, does little or nothing to improve sales performance. That requires not just knowledge, but action.

Both Celebrate Hunting

Our earliest ancestors of the Paleolithic period relied exclusively on hunting for their survival (Armstrong 2005, chap. 2). Agriculture as a source of food had not yet evolved. Hunters of this ancient period put their lives at risk to track down and kill larger, stronger prey and ultimately bring food back to their people. Priests gave the hunt spiritual meaning, as important as weapons and skills to their success.

Hunting is a common metaphor for selling today. On Wall Street, a successful salesman will announce a major win by proclaiming to the rest of the floor that he *shot an elephant*. In other industries, salespeople will leave the safety of their offices days at a time, just like their Paleolithic ancestors left the security of their caves, to go *hunting* for more business. Some businesses that operate exclusively on a commission basis, refer to it as an *eat what you kill* system. Indeed, the very existence of contemporary businesses is dependent upon the performance of their sales teams, just as people of the Paleolithic period were dependent upon their hunters.

Live Sacrifices

Ancient cultures offered sacrifices like live animals to their mythological gods. Today's *rainmakers* demand and receive cars, bonuses, vacations, and expense accounts in order to out *schmooze* their adversaries. The motivation to appease the mythological gods and the rainmakers is the same: fear. The ancient Greeks feared that angry gods were behind cruel weather conditions. Business organizations that are dependent on rainmakers today appease them with lavish perquisites, lest they leave and take key clients with them.

A Little Truth

There is a little bit of truth in mythology. Most mythical heroes were real people whose accomplishments became exaggerated each time the feats were retold. For example, most agree that George Washington was a great American president. But no one, not even George Washington, could throw a silver dollar across the Delaware River.

Similarly, there's a bit of truth in each of the sales myths. In fact, some people have natural interpersonal gifts and are skilled at relating to people. When they build business relationships, they can *make it rain*. Schmooze can indeed help provide opportunities where business relationships can be cemented. While an emphasis on closing has been shown to have an inverse impact on success in major and complex selling, good salespeople always have a sense of *milestones* (developed in Chapter Ten) and relentlessly pursue the next steps after every selling initiative.

In the movie *Field of Dreams,* Kevin Costner's character was assured that, if he built a baseball diamond, *they will come*. While buyers will not just emerge from the cornfields as the Black Socks did in *Field of Dreams,* having an excellent product certainly helps.

WHAT'S WRONG WITH MYTHS

What then is wrong with believing in myths? They have, after all, been a part of human history since the beginning of time. Mythology has exerted a powerful influence on our cultures, the arts, and the way we think. Even the eminent psychiatrist Carl Jung had a place for mythology, believing it played a prominent role in our *collective unconscious*.

The answer for businesses is that a reliance on myths leads to sub-optimal performance at best and, in the worse case, to extinction. Subscribing to myths can lead to looking for rainmakers and hiring the wrong people. Believing that *closing* is a crucial selling skill can prompt the wrong training initiatives and result in a sales force using techniques that actually discourage buying behaviors. Beta VCRs, Xerox copiers, and Apple computers reveal the hazards of the *Field of Dreams* myth. While they all had superior products to their competitors, Beta is now extinct and Xerox and Apple are mere shadows of what they once were.

Many companies waste untold dollars on *schmoozing* their clients rather than teaching and reinforcing the right skills and disciplines that comprise a comprehensive sales system. They allow their sales teams to roam without regard to discipline or process. In short, subscribing to myths encourages the kinds of behaviors that would never be tolerated in other parts of the organization where the resident gods are logic and reason.

A SYSTEMATIC APPROACH TO SELLING

Rather than relying on myths, businesses need to approach selling with the same rigor they apply when making or delivering their products. Changing a

Strategy

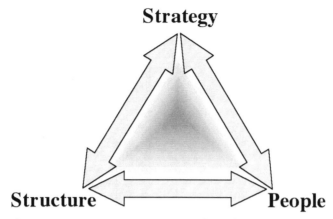

Structure   People

Figure 1.1.   Strategy, Structure & People Model

sales culture dependent upon myths is not an easy course. After all, the ancient Greeks continued to believe in myths for hundreds of years after Plato pointed out their falsehoods in *The Republic*.

Challenging modern sales myths that seem to be supported by conventional wisdom can be tricky business. Sometimes bright and respected people promulgate them. Like Plato, we seek to debunk sales myths in section one by drawing distinctions between the logic that exposes them and the popular opinion that sustains them. Wherever possible, we draw upon a growing body of hard evidence supporting a more rational and systematic approach to selling.

One of the reasons ancient cultures relied on myths to explain hard to understand phenomena is that they didn't have an alternate explanation. Sections two through four are dedicated to a rational model for a process approach to selling: *Strategy, Structure and People*™. All three need to be in place. It begins with a smart strategy that is effectively translated throughout the organization. Structure follows strategy. It then measures and rewards the right behaviors and not the residual ones from an old culture. Selling is done in a replicable fashion driven by a process approach and not reliant on Rainmakers, Closers, Schmooze, or Field of Dreams myths. The *Strategy, Structure & People* ™ model is the key to emancipating selling from mythology and the transformation to a logical, scientific, and higher performing approach to selling.

Chapter Two

Rainmakers

Mythological worship of natural forces transcends many cultures including African, Greek, Scandinavian, and Native American. The ceremonies and rituals of the latter, however, are the source for the modern term *rainmaker.*

NATIVE AMERICAN RAIN DANCES

Inhabiting the desert of the American southwest, Hopi have coped successfully with the natural rigors of their region. Central to their culture is the worship of the sun, fire, and rain. Rain dances are conducted with live snakes to petition the gods to bring rain and ensure a good harvest. The men who perform the Snake Dance are powerful figures in the Hopi culture believed to have special powers essential to the tribes' survival. (Wilkinson 1998).

RAINMAKERS

The Hopi practice likely influenced a breed of less honorable *rainmakers* who roamed the dust bowl in the 1930s promising rain in exchange for money. Burt Lancaster and Katharine Hepburn starred in a film adaptation of the N. Richard Nash play, *The Rainmaker*. Lancaster plays Starbuck, a con man who shows up at the drought ridden Curry farm and offers to make it rain for $100. Starbuck doesn't propose to do the Snake Dance, just to apply his charismatic capabilities to coax rain from the skies.

In a classic exchange, farm owner H. C. Curry proclaims that he doesn't believe in rainmakers. To which Starbuck replies, "What do you believe in Mister? Dying cattle?"

Today, *rainmaker* is a term used to connote someone who has special, natural, god-given talents to ensure the welfare of the business culture by bringing it what it needs to survive: new business. Whether it is accomplished with snakes or charisma matters little as long as it rains. Rest assured that no CEO or managing partner wants to head to a board meeting to explain the business equivalent of dying cattle.

SALESMEN ARE BORN. NOT MADE.

The great risk of the Rainmaker myth is holding the belief that selling skills are something you either have or don't have. To the contrary, we contend that mere mortals can learn the skills and follow the disciplines necessary to succeed in major and complex selling.

The opening scene of *Glengarry GlenRoss*, the 1992 film adapted from David Mamet's Pulitzer Prize winning play, is instructive. Alec Baldwin plays the role of a rainmaker brought in by real estate developers, Mitch and Murray to motivate their under-performing sales team. The group is comprised of characters portrayed by Alan Arkin, Ed Harris, and Jack Lemmon. Their lone exemplary performer, played by Al Pacino, skips the meeting to set a trap for an unsuspecting mark he meets in a bar.

While Baldwin's character excoriates them for not being "men enough" to sell, a sign hangs over the sales manager's office (played by Kevin Spacey) that reads:

Salesmen are born. Not made

The essence of the Rainmaker myth is in that sign.

What are the natural attributes found in rainmakers? The images cut by these two classic films, *The Rainmaker* and *Glengarry GlenRoss*, while unflattering, are indeed representative. Burt Lancaster's Starbuck suggests that charisma and talents for conning are what it takes to sell. Alec Baldwin's Blake would have us believe that it is all about testosterone. As he poses this rhetorical question, "You know what it takes to sell real estate?" he reaches into his open briefcase and dangles a pair of brass balls in front of his crotch. Reinforcing his visual aid, Blake answers his own question. "It takes brass balls to sell real estate."

Our research, and that of others like Neil Rackham, consistently shows that, while charisma never hurt anyone in any field, success in selling is neither about conning nor testosterone. It is all about skills like questioning, listening, developing a comprehensive buyer profile, customizing communication and negotiating. It also requires the discipline to apply those skills. Even highly charismatic types don't last, if they lack the requisite skills and discipline for selling.

RISKS OF BELIEVING IN RAINMAKERS

With apologies to the Hopis and the dust bowl farmers who bought rainmaking promises, subscribing to the Rainmaker myth can be disastrous. A modern day Snake Dance is just not a smart model for business or professional practice growth. Paradoxically, the use of the term is most common in professional practices like law and accounting.

Subscribing to the Rainmaker myth:

- Stymies attempts to teach the skills, provide the tools, and set a good sales process in place
- Encourages recruitment and selection of those with mythical rainmaker attributes, i.e. charisma, conning, and testosterone
- Discourages those who perceive themselves to be mere mortals from succeeding in selling
- Encourages those who are pegged as rainmakers to extract extra perquisites from their organizations
- Allows clients to focus on individual relationships with rainmakers instead of on the business-to-business level
- Sets the stage for rainmakers to hold the organization hostage by threatening to take accounts with them

"I DON'T BELIEVE IN RAINMAKERS."

In debunking the Rainmaker myth, we side with the sentiments of farmer H. C. Curry when he said, "I don't believe in rainmakers." And we take exception to the sign hanging over the sales manager's office and the views espoused by Blake in *Glengarry GlenRoss* .

We assert that people are not born to be salespeople anymore than they are born to be geologists, language teachers, or oyster shuckers. While there are natural talents, selling skills can be learned. And the perpetuation of the Rainmaker myth does a grave disservice to anyone who was discouraged from the field because they were not born with a *rainmaking* personality.

SCORECARD

1. Do you use the term *rainmaker* for top-performing salespeople in your organization?

2. Does your firm hold the view that, *"Well, some of us can do this and some of us can't"?*
3. Do you afford special privileges to those who can *make it rain?*
4. Have you had an executive level conference recently about the need to hire some rainmakers?
5. Is the work of your organization highly technical, performed by licensed or certified professionals?
6. Do the high-performing technical experts harbor a view, private or public, that the work they do is more important than selling?
7. Does your organization aspire to become so well known and respected that, someday, you won't have to rely on rainmakers.
8. Does your organization believe that salespeople are just affable, back slapping guys (generic, of course) who had low GPAs in college and now play a lot of golf?

Chapter Three

Closers

AS SIMPLE AS ABC

Movie classic *Glengarry GlenRoss* is also instructive in debunking sales myth number two: Closers. In the opening scene, just as Blake (played by Alec Baldwin) is launching his tirade, Shelly "The Machine" Levine (played by Jack Lemmon) gets up and walks over to the coffee pot. Blake confronts the startled Levine with what has become the most repeated line from the film:

"Put that coffee down! Coffee is for closers."

After leveling Levine, Blake turns to a blackboard and writes this simple formula for selling success:

A - Always
B - Be
C - Closing

Always Be Closing!

CLOSING TECHNIQUES

In *Glengarry GlenRoss* art imitates life. Closing had been the cornerstone of sales training programs for many years. The best companies in the world have emphasized closing techniques and sometimes its first cousin, *handling objections*. In the early 1990s, our firm worked with a Fortune 100 company whose core sales training was two weeks of memorizing closing scripts. There were 62 of them. If script number one didn't work, they were trained to use another. If number two didn't produce the close, it was on to yet another, ad nauseam. What makes this even scarier, is that it was representative of the prevailing approach to sales training, even among the biggest and the best companies in the world — IBM, Xerox, Exxon, GTE, Kodak.

Sales literature is rife with closing techniques. There are the basic ones like the Alternative Close (*Would you like it in red or green?*); the Assumptive Close (*Would you like deliveries on Mondays or Tuesdays?*); the Take-away (*You can't have it because someone else wants it*); the Puppy Dog (*Take it home and you'll want to have it, just like a puppy dog*); the Last Chance (*This is the last one at this price*); the Ben Franklin (*List, then analyze all of the reasons to buy, and knock down all of the ones not to buy.*); and the Order Blank (*The salesperson fills out an order form even though the prospect has never indicated a desire to buy*).

There is even a book with this compelling title, *101 Sure Fire Ways to Irresistibly Close Any Sale*. The operative words are, of course, *irresistible* and *any*. After all, who could resist closing techniques with names like the Speed Bump (*Get them to rattle off one yes after another, like hitting speed bumps*); the Future (*Let's just fill out the paperwork and then work on the details sometime in the future*); the Killer Close (Mercifully, this one doesn't threaten bodily harm. It's just a version of the Alternative Close).

Pretty hideous, isn't it?

THE FAB TO CLOSE MODEL

The *close* is the last step in the long taught and, in some corners, still revered *FAB to Close* model. Fundamentally, this approach emphasizes pitching product Features, Advantages and Benefits (FAB), skillfully handling objections, and then going for the kill with a clever closing script. The FAB to Close approach is illustrated below:

Even if you have never sold, you are, we are sure, familiar with FAB to Close because you have been on the receiving end as buyers. Daily encounters with telemarketers represent one small dose.

There is just one problem with closing techniques. They don't work. Closing is a sales myth.

RACKHAM THE HERETIC

In the mid-1980s, enlightened businesses were growing skeptical of their own training programs. While the FAB to Close model seemed to work with commodity level buyers, it yielded disappointing results at a higher order sale with more sophisticated clients.

What wasn't known was what skills *did work* at the major and complex level. They turned to researcher Neil Rackham to uncover the answer.

Rackham (1988) and his team launched what turned out to be a twelve-year study. They investigated 35,000 calls where they observed and evaluated the outcomes of sales techniques. They observed sales practices of star performers, typical performers, and disappointing ones over a wide array of industries.

Here's what they found: "Our research shows convincingly that, in larger sales at least, the use of closing techniques is negatively related to success." (Rackham 1988, 28)

Simply put, Rackham and his team found that the more salespeople used closing techniques, the less likely it was for them to succeed. Among the analyses they performed was a study where they compared the performance of one group, trained in closing, against another not trained in that approach. The performance of the group implementing their new closing skills performed at a lower rate than the group without it.

CLOSING ZEALOTS

The priests reacted in a predictable fashion. They were furious. Heresy they shouted, of course closing works. Just ask experienced salespeople. Rackham (1988, 37) even tells the story of being pulled off a stage by an angry sales trainer when reporting his findings that the more people tried closing techniques the less likely they were to win a sale. Interestingly, he reinforces our *myth–priest* metaphor by describing the conviction of many salespeople to closing as "almost a religion." (Rackham 1988, 37)

The priests promoting the myth of closing were ready to punish the mere mortal Rackham for his sacrilegious views. Like the ancient priests advancing Greek mythology, they fought with dogma and opinion. Like the rationalists who preceded him, Rackham fought back with empirical research and science. The fight goes on.

OUR EVIDENCE

We were invited to make a proposal to provide training for a sales force numbering sixty. The vice president of sales and marketing was certain that deficient selling skills were the reason why his team was not performing at the level expected.

We were not the first solution he had tried. The previous firm, touting pedigrees as former sales trainers from household name firms, had presented a FAB to Close program. It didn't work. Sales remained flat.

Sporting some healthy and understandable skepticism, he offered us an opportunity to start with a group of ten for whom performance would be measured against the remaining fifty. Data would be gathered for a quarter. Being sales guys ourselves, we argued for the whole pie, but we were restricted to just a slice, to start.

The restriction turned out to be fortuitous. We had a classic *experimental* group (the 10 with our SST®: Successful Selling to Type program) versus a *control* group (the remaining 50 practicing FAB to Close) study.

Three months later the experimental group (those with the skills we taught) had out-performed the control group (the Closers) by 483%. Our only problem was that the results were so severe they would sound incredible to some. If you are a doubter, we can provide the hard data. (ajtilden@ tildensst.com)

We also conduct studies that are more qualitative in character. For example, when we do an Exemplary Performer Analysis, we interview star performers and compare their skills, methods and tools to more typical performers. In the dozens of studies we have done with hundreds of exemplary performers, we have never come across one who attributed his or her success to superior closing skills.

With apologies to the gods, priests, and poets of the Closer myth, we have never interviewed an exemplary performing salesperson who said his or her success was due to *The Ben Franklin, The Takeaway,* or *The Speed Bump Close*. Nor have we heard about *The Double Whammy Reverse* technique in these interviews.

THE MYTH THAT WON'T DIE

Debunking the Closer myth is perhaps the trickiest one of all. Rackham's research, reported in *SPIN Selling* (1988), should have killed it. We can assure you, however, that a lot of salespeople did not attend the funeral. Just recently, we heard this from a frustrated sales manager, "We give them all these resources from laptops with PowerPoint presentations to Blackberries. They're still afraid to ask for the sale. They just don't know how to close!"

Now, this is from a bright guy with a Fortune 100 firm. Further, it has been fifteen years since Rackham's findings were reported. How does the closing myth avoid death more deftly than Count Dracula? As Rackham (1988, 37-38) recounts, the answer in part can be traced to what is done *last* in the sales process, or what psychologists refer to as the *recency effect*. It comes into play when trying to put the closing myth to rest.

Here's what we mean: Let's say that an account executive does a marvelous job at the investigation stage of the process. She researches her prospect before the call. She plans and asks good questions. Then she listens carefully to identify a problem and all of its implications. Since this a major and complex setting, she asks permission to have a follow-up appointment to propose solutions to the problem.

Meanwhile, she not only prepares the technical content to the solution, she takes care to package the message to appeal to all communication styles that will be attending the follow-up meeting. She has strategies for all of the different buyer influences. Her proposal is customized, concise, and engaging. The buying signals are clear. Then she asks, "Would you like to start with our solution in October or early November?" They say early November.

Delighted with the outcome she rushes back to tell her sales manager. "We won!" she declares. "I asked if they wanted to start in October or November. That alternative close technique works like magic!" Since the sales manager is a closing zealot himself, he responds by saying, "Great going. You are a real closer!"

And the Closer myth endures.

People tend to associate what they did *last* as the cause of getting the desired result when, in fact, there is a series of behaviors that led up to it. In selling, it has to do with behaviors like planning and asking good questions, presenting customized solutions, and executing an effective strategy for all of the decision influences.

And, of course, there is the semantic problem with the word *close*. It has become synonymous with *success*, *sale,* and *win*. When we ask sales managers and other executives what result they would most like to see from a sales training initiative, many will say better *closing*. This is truly an instance when you better be careful of what you wish for. Better closing skills will not produce more *successes*, *sales* and *wins*. You will get fewer.

IF NOT CLOSING, WHAT WORKS?

If it's not closing that works, what does? Rather than the clever closing scripts that were being memorized, Rackham found that the common denominator in successful major and complex sales was asking good questions. "There's no doubt about it, questions persuade more powerfully than any other form of verbal behavior" (Rackham 1988, 14).[1]

Ironically, the skills that are truly related to successful selling are those that have to do with opening the sales with effective questioning, rather than closing with a clever manipulation. It is the whole sequence of behaviors described with our hypothetical salesperson—from conducting a good investigation, to customizing communication, to managing multiple buyer influences—that make for successful selling. The alternative close may not have hurt, but by itself would not have led to a win. Since it was done last, however, many closing zealots believe that it caused the sale. They are the snake dancers and sun worshipers of modern selling.

SCORECARD

1. Do you conduct training programs that emphasize closing skills?
2. Do you use the term *close* as a synonym for *win*?
3. In forecasting sales through pipelines or sales funnels, do you put an emphasis on the latter stages of the sales cycle?
4. Are salespeople scripted with closing techniques?
5. When you are recruiting salespeople do you intentionally look for *closing* abilities?

Chapter Four

Schmooze

We were doing an Exemplary Performer Analysis for a prominent Wall Street investment bank. The essence of this form of research is to identify behaviors, characteristics, or activities demonstrated by star or *exemplary* performers that contribute to their success and distinguish them from *typical* performers.

We asked this question, "The last time you had a major selling success, what was the key factor?"

Predictably, everyone we interviewed responded with the same answer: "Relationships," they said.

The answers to our next question, however, clearly differentiated the *exemplary* performers from their more *typical* counterparts. When we queried as to how salespeople build productive business relationships, the typical performers answered with a loud, uniform, and resounding:

"Schmooze!"

THE MOST COVETED AND MOST DEMEANING MYTH

Myth three is one embraced by salespeople, prospects, and clients alike. After all, who wouldn't like free tickets to the game, tournament, or show? What golfer wouldn't love to see a major tournament and be wined and dined at a well-stocked hospitality tent?

The myth persists for obvious reasons. While the cold calling, rejection, waiting, report writing, and boring meetings are all arduous dimensions of the sales racket, the schmooze is great. Many salespeople would sooner surrender a first born than give up schmooze. Prospects and clients love it just as much, if not more.

Challenging the institution of schmooze is a prescription for being barraged with emotional appeals of its effectiveness substantiated by anecdotes where it was instrumental in landing a big account. And if you still haven't acquiesced, you are sure to be pounded with chapter and verse of accounts lost to competitors who simply out-schmoozed the rest of the field.

While it is the most coveted myth, it is also the most demeaning to the sales field. Sales performers blinded by the power of schmooze are acknowledging that they don't know how buying decisions get made. Like the ancient societies who gave elaborate gifts to mythical gods, modern business organizations that don't understand selling invest huge sums of money to appease existing clients and woo prospective ones.

SALES PROFESSIONALS?

At the risk of sounding esoteric, we are reluctant to use the term *professional* in connection with selling. This shouldn't suggest that we don't believe it to be an admirable or significant field. It is, after all, what we teach and do.

The term *professional* does, however, carry a technical meaning that we respect. Professionals are licensed by the state or certified by a professional organization setting standards for the practice. Therefore, we intentionally narrow the scope of the term to fields like accounting, architecture, law, and medicine.

Be that as it may, can you imagine buyers making significant *professional* decisions based solely on schmooze? Faced with a significant health problem, would any buyer be ultimately influenced by the physician or surgeon who *schmoozed* him or her the best? Or, would any intelligent consumer choose one attorney over another because he or she offered better seats at the ball game?

The careful reader of the above paragraph will have picked up on three important caveats: *solely, ultimately,* and *intelligent.* They are fitting because, like all of the four sales myths, there is a bit of truth to schmooze.

If other things are equal, most would choose the attorney who sponsors an annual golf outing. But when the matter boils down to issues like trust, expertise, and competency, schmooze goes out the window as a decision factor in professional settings.

NEVER A SUBSTITUTE FOR PROCESS

We consistently find that organizations overly reliant on the Schmooze myth fail to have a rigorous sales process in place. As a result, serious buying decisions tend to go to the competitors who, in addition to schmooze, have demonstrated a capacity to understand the client's problems and build a business relationship positioning their skills and competencies at delivering solutions to those problems. At crunch time, the call will always go to the firm that can solve problems over the one that can deliver tickets.

WHAT EXEMPLARY SALES PERFORMERS DO

Let's return to the Exemplary Performer Analysis we conducted for our Wall Street client comparing selling stars to more typical performers. While the typical performers in our study all relied on schmooze, the exemplary ones revealed a more sophisticated understanding of what it takes to build meaningful business relationships. While no one in their right mind would suggest that schmooze be phased out, the exemplary performers treat schmooze for what it's worth: social opportunities that afford an occasion to get to know a client or prospect a little better, socially. Many indicate that they make it a point never to discuss business issues during schmoozing activities. They separate social schmooze from serious business, which puts them and their clients at ease. Nothing is tackier than a young schlepper hitting on a client for business when he is trying to choose the right club for a difficult shot into the wind and over water.

Instead, exemplary performers reported that they relied on a *process* (whether they used that precise term or not). While there is considerable room for different personal styles, there are common elements to the processes exemplary performers apply. We will develop these elements more fully in subsequent chapters, but all exemplary performers follow a process where they move from one milestone to the next (developed more fully in Chapter Ten).

If you or your organization depend too heavily on schmooze at the expense of a rigorous sales process, your clients and prospects will consistently go to your competitors when the moment of truth rolls around. While schmooze might help break a tie, it is never a substitute for excellence in product design and delivery, nor does it replace the rigors of a systematic approach to selling.

SCORECARD

1. Do you dedicate more than ten percent of your sales budget to entertaining clients and other schmoozing?

2. When you host functions like golf or ski outings, do you refer to them as business or practice development?
3. Do you spend the same or more on schmoozing than you do on training and skill building?
4. Do you have a shared and replicable sales system that outlines significant steps and milestones?
5. Do you monitor pipeline or sales funnel activities to forecast sales?

Chapter Five

Field of Dreams

THE GHOSTS LIED

In the movie *Field of Dreams,* baseball-playing ghosts instruct Kevin Costner's character to proceed and build a baseball field because "If you build it, they will come."

This mantra seems to be the myth behind many failed, failing, and under-performing enterprises. Marquee names like Apple Computer, Beta video recorders, and Xerox office equipment are among them. If you asked top executives at any one of those organizations, they would tell you the same thing. The ghosts lied. Just building a superior computer, video recorder, or copier does not mean that customers will come.

"If you build it, they will come" is sales myth number four. We call it *Field of Dreams.*

XEROX

Xerox was once such a dominant force in the copying industry that its very name became synonymous with making photocopies. *"Let me Xerox a copy for you"* was a common business expression for making duplicate copies.

Although Xerox is recovering from a near financial collapse in the early 2000s, it is a mere shadow of its former self. This slow and painful recovery (especially for more than 14,000 laid off workers) is not due to the quality of the copiers it manufactures.

One of the main contributors to the Xerox decline can be traced to how it reorganized its sales force. To put this in perspective, Xerox once had the sales training model emulated by every major sales organization. Salespeople would list the Xerox Professional Selling Skills sales training on their resumes with Ivy League kind of pride. To have the sales function at Xerox move from admired strength to a serious weakness is a terrible business irony.

In an effort to streamline its operations, Xerox moved from a geographic structure to one based on industries. Many long-term relationships were disrupted, which served to alienate customers. Sensing a golden opportunity, competitors like Ricoh and Canon have moved in on long-time Xerox clients with a vengeance.

Ricoh's president, Jim Ivy is quoted in a *New York Times* article (October 18, 2000) as follows, "Xerox has annoyed its customers and its employees and that's giving us one of our best years ever." At the time of the quote, Ricoh had taken more than 14 percent of the copier market from Xerox.

"If you build it, they will come." Ask ousted Xerox CEO, G. Richard Thoman if it is enough to have superior copier machines and brand name recognition once the envy of every Fortune 100 Company. If you muck around with the sales organization and disrupt long-term interpersonal relationships, they will not come. They will go to a competitor.

Wall Street giant Xerox almost came undone by its reliance on the Field of Dreams myth. It has a lot of company from the Fortune 100 level right down to Mom & Pops and Two Bobs with a Truck. Regardless of size and market dominance, care needs to be taken that the sales function is pursued with the same careful planning, intelligence, and rigor that is applied to manufacturing the product or delivering the service.

SHINIER BELLS & LOUDER WHISTLES

For those hooked on the Field of Dreams myth, there is often an engineering corollary that unfolds when sales are disappointing. Convinced that hard differentiators are the only ones that matter, these organizations will turn to engineers in search of a *shinier bell*.

Once again, Xerox serves as an example. They invented the copying machine and few products saw more success or faster growth. But pursuing shinier bells or louder whistles, they consistently added features as the path to continued growth.

Management guru Peter Drucker (2005, 171-172) observed that many of Xerox's smaller customers had little to no need for the features that came with high end machines and were content with the simple efficiencies of copying pages. Japanese competitors sensed the disillusionment in this market segment and designed simple, reasonably priced copy machines, ones without bells or whistles, and quickly gained market share.

The U.S. automobile industry is another prime example of the shinier bell delusion. For years, the Big Three (GM, Ford & Chrysler) would roll out hard differentiators like "rack and pinion" steering or "rich Corinthian leather".

Meanwhile, Japanese auto manufacturers were focusing on quality and fuel efficiency. What will it be: shinier bells or better quality? Would you prefer a louder whistles or more miles to the gallon? Many customers don't care or even know what rack and pinion steering is and *rich Corinthian leather* turns out to be a made-up term. Organizations that pursue shinier bells and louder whistles are sentenced to the same fates as Xerox, GM, and Ford.

FIELD OF DREAMS DEBUNKED

No one contends that great products are not important. But by themselves, without matching rigor and discipline in the sales and marketing function, an organization will never have optimal performance.

Soft differentiators often make the hard difference in sales performance. This is especially true at the consultative level of selling. By definition, when a buyer is functioning in a commodity market, he knows all he needs to know about the product. Great selling skills don't matter at this level. Here, it is all about the quality of the mousetrap.

At the consultative level, however, sales decisions have more to do with the trust the buyer has in the salesperson's skill and expertise in helping them find a solution to a problem. Whether the consultative salesperson uses hard differentiator A or B is secondary to the trusting relationship that is built.

It is analogous to a patient-physician relationship. In choosing a surgeon, patients care more about the trust they have in the doctor's skills and expertise than the hospital where the operation will be conducted. Those who subscribe to the Field of Dreams myth behave as though only the hospital matters. Even worse, salespeople who push the shinier bells on their products are doing precisely the wrong kinds of things to build the kind of trusting relationships Xerox once had and then threw away to *streamline* their organization.

Once again, the answer for exemplary sales performance is not found in the Field of Dreams myth. Nor will it be discovered pursuing myths like Rainmakers, Closers or Schmooze. Rather, the solution is in an integrated system that coordinates *Strategy, Structure and People*™, summarized in the next chapter.

SCORECARD

1. Is your business development strategy to *out-engineer* the competition?
2. Are salespeople assigned second-class, or necessary evil status in the organization?
3. Does your sales training emphasize technical product knowledge over selling skills?
4. Do you neglect to use salespeople as a source of market intelligence?
5. Are your salespeople trained in a replicable sales process with milestones that can be plotted in a pipeline?

Chapter Six

An Integrated System Not Myth

Some advertising tag lines stick with us for generations. No doubt you will be able to fill in the blanks in the following examples:

- Winston tastes good. . . .
- When you absolutely, positively, have to. . . .
- The system is . . .

Indeed, the system *is* the solution. The solution is not found in blindly sub-scribing to one or more of the four sales myths: Rainmakers, Closers, Schmooze, or Field of Dreams.

Organizations seeking optimum sales performance will find it in a system-atic approach to selling characterized by all of the rigor and discipline typi-cally invested in manufacturing quality products or in delivering superb ser-vices. With a system in place, the organization can choose the right talent and teach the right skills to a sales team. No longer does it need to be held hostage to mythological heroes who claim to be born with the ability to make it rain.

Three business functions need to be synchronized to form a system[1]. They are *Strategy, Structure and People*™. All top-performing sales organizations are characterized by:

1. Smart strategy that is translated throughout the organization
2. A structure that fits the strategy
3. People who possess the right talents and skills to execute a replicable sales process[2]. A smart strategy with an old culture structure will never yield op-timum results, nor will a new structure inhabited by people with the wrong talents and skills.

Too often, organizations hold the myopic view that performance improvement can be accomplished by investing in one or two of the three components, naively believing that the other one or two will fall in place. Optimum performance requires attention to all three business functions: *Strategy, Structure & People*™. They are illustrated below:

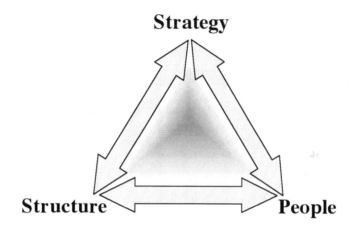

Strategy

Structure   People

STRATEGY

We believe war to be an apt metaphor for strategy. This is particularly true for sales strategies where there are enemies and failure results in dire consequences, like extinction, to both organizations and the people who inhabit them. We draw upon the ancient and still insightful, *The Art of War* by Sun Tzu, to develop our views of what it takes to have effective strategy. It must be coordinated and function from the very top of the organization right down to where the sales force is engaged in hand-to-hand combat. This is the topic for *Chapter Seven: Wage War-Win Business.*

High-performing organizations differ from more typical ones in how they do strategic planning. Those differences are itemized in *Chapter Eight: What Strategy Is and Is Not.*

Before an enemy is engaged in battle, and analogously, before salespeople are sent into to the field, the attack needs to be planned. For selling, this means analyzing the buying modes in which customers are functioning: transactional, consultative, or enterprise. The way value is added for the client varies with each and determines which sales process should be pursued. The Rackham & DeVincentis buying mode paradigm is explicated in *Chapter Nine: Three Ways to Create Value-Three Types of Sales.* This model should guide market segmentation, rather than the common segmenting schemes based on size or geography.

Chapter Ten: Process Driven Selling focuses on the level of strategy where sales managers function. Their single most important obligation is to guide their sales teams in a replicable process characterized by milestones that represent important and measurable steps to winning a consultative sale. Milestones can be plotted in a pipeline, which is an indispensable sales performance tool for both sales managers and salespeople.

STRUCTURE

Smart strategy is never enough to achieve optimum sales performance. It must be supported by a formal structure that: measures the right things, rewards the right behaviors, renders consequences for the wrong ones, and allocates resources to support the strategy. These topics are addressed in *Chapter Eleven: Formal Structure*.

While formal structures can be illustrated in public organization charts, they only tell part of the story. *The Informal Structure* (Chapter Twelve) has to do with assumptions, values, informal rewards, and *psychological contracts,* the terms of which are perpetuated over beverages like coffee and beer. It is a naive leader who believes he or she can implement a new strategy by only engaging the formal aspects of an organization. They need to co-opt informal leaders and manage psychological contracts as well.

PEOPLE

Having a smart strategy and a structure that supports it are still not enough to achieve exemplary performance. That structure needs to be inhabited by people with the requisite *talents* and *skills* to implement the strategy. The former are natural god-given attributes and they, not skills, should be the priority for recruiting and selection as treated in *Chapter Thirteen: Recruit for Talents*.

Chapter Fourteen: The Recruiting Pipeline provides a tool that will enable managers to move quickly when the inevitable critical opening occurs on a sales team, one where competitors are anxious to move in and gain market share.

While Chapter Thirteen deals with talents that should be spotlighted during recruitment and selection, Chapter Fifteen focuses on the second half of what should be a sales management mantra: *Recruit for Talents, Train for Skills.* It brings forward the hypothetical sales process delineated in Chapter

Ten and illustrates why it is crucial for sales to follow the sales process unique to every business. *Chapter Fifteen: Train for Skills* concludes with an annotation of four sales skills building programs that will add value to any consultative sales skill training (SPIN Selling, The Know What, How & Why Questioning Model, Multiple Decision Influences and SST®: Successful Selling to Type.

Chapter Sixteen addresses a new sales myth that is emerging: *Automation.* Many otherwise smart companies are investing large sums of money in CRM (Customer Relationship Management) or SFA (Sales Force Automation) with disappointing results. The explanation is quite simple: process should always precede automation. Without a process in place first, expensive CRM or SFA only serve to exaggerate, rather than solve sales performance problems.

The remainder of this book is intended to be a resource for what needs to be done to improve sales performance by adopting an integrated system, one that embraces issues pertaining to *Strategy, Structure and People*™. Questions similar to the ones appearing below will be listed at the conclusion of each chapter. While the *Scorecard* questions should put a spotlight on the *knowledge* of what needs to be done, that is not enough without a commitment to specific *actions*. The concluding chapter of this book, *Chapter Seventeen: Plan of Action,* will provide guidelines on what the reader needs to *do* to improve individual or team level sales performance.

SCORECARD

1. If we asked people to summarize your strategy, would they be able to?
2. If we asked three different people with similar responsibilities to summarize the strategy, would we get three different answers?
3. If we asked leaders to state the terms of the psychological contract, would they be able to? (*If we do this, we get that.*)
4. If we asked leaders to list the intrinsic rewards that are delivered in your organization, would they be able to?
5. Do the intrinsic rewards reinforce desired behaviors?
6. Did you address cultural barriers in implementing your plan?
7. If we asked three salespeople to outline their selling process, would we get three different answers?
8. Are you able to list the milestones in your sales process?
9. Do you use a pipeline or funnel to track and forecast new sales?
10. Do you have a sales training curriculum organized around the requisite skills at each milestone in the pipeline

11. If we asked sales leaders to profile the talents and skills necessary to excel at sales in your organization, would there be a common list?
12. Do you recruit for talent and train for skills?

NOTES

1. For the purposes of this manuscript, *system* refers to the *Strategy, Structure & People*™ model.

2. For the purposes of this manuscript, *process* refers to milestones comprising the sales pipeline treated in Chapter Ten.

Section Two

STRATEGY

"The general who wins a battle does many calculations before the battle is fought. The general who loses a battle makes but few calculations beforehand. Thus do many calculations lead to victory and few calculations to defeat."

Sun Tzu

Chapter Seven

Wage War-Win Business

The metaphor of business strategy as war is an increasingly popular one, with many leaders relying on the ancient wisdom of Sun Tzu in *The Art of War,* written nearly 2000 years ago. While strategic planning needs to go on everywhere in an organization, it is the market facing sales function where the *business is war* metaphor is the best fit:

- There are enemies
- Competitors want the same thing: more business
- There are winners and losers
- Winners always have the better strategy
- Strategy guides execution
- Sometimes the tactics are ruthless
- The stakes are high
- Losers endure human and economic consequences.

Further, the metaphor of war helps us understand the different levels at which sales strategy is determined. Sun Tzu wrote (Sawyer 1994) that war should be planned at four different levels:

1. Sovereigns
2. Generals
3. Officers
4. Soldiers

SOVEREIGNS

Sovereigns, of course, are heads of state: monarchs, prime ministers, presidents and the like. They correspond in business organizations to boards of directors. Here, policy is set at a global level. Determinations are made as to whom war will be waged against and with whom alliances will be formed. The costs and benefits of waging war for the people they represent are assessed. For sovereigns, the welfare of countrymen should be paramount. Once the decision to go to war has been made, the most important decision sovereigns make is choosing generals.

The parallels to business should be clear. Instead of countrymen, boards are looking out for the welfare of shareholders and the performance of stocks and dividends they earn. Determinations of product mix and market share goals are decisions that should be sanctioned in the boardroom. The most important decision boards make is choosing the CEO, who often sits on the board and chooses his or her staff of generals.

Directors help set or sanction the long-term strategic direction of the organization. And like kings and queens, boards of directors examine the competitive landscape in the broad sense and approve strategic alliances. Sometimes they even get royal treatment.

GENERALS

Generals hold top military rank and set strategy at the highest levels. They plan and coordinate attacks from the ground, sea, and air. Generals also choose and, when necessary, fire their officers. In business, generals wear titles like CEO, president, vice president, partner and managing director. They lead different parts of the organization like operations, human resources, and sales. The departments they lead need to function in a synchronized fashion to win a battle in business, just as armies and navies need to be coordinated in war.

Classic strategic planning is conducted at this level, including an assessment of internal Strengths and Weaknesses and external Opportunities and Threats (SWOT). The planning done by generals is communicated upward to the board where it is sanctioned. Markets are segmented to guide sales managers and sales personnel. This should include the identification of key accounts and their characteristics.

Too frequently, market segmentation is determined by product characteristics, or what Charan & Tichy (1998) call an *inside-out* perspective. Rather, market segmentation should be driven from the *outside-in* focusing on the needs of customers and clients and the value provided by a product. "Look from the outside in. Reach into the customers' thoughts, see their needs and work backward. That's the fundamental lesson. Everything else is execution." (Charan & Tichy 1998, 70)

Similarly, Sun Tzu cited the wisdom of looking both inward and outward when he said:

> Knowing that the enemy can be attacked, and knowing that our army can effect the attack, but not knowing the terrain is not suitable for combat, is only halfway to victory. Thus one who truly knows the army will never be deluded when he moves, never be impoverished when initiating an action.
>
> Thus it is said if you know them and know yourself, your victory will not be imperiled.

> (Sawyer 1994, 135)

Ancient generals and modern sales leaders alike need to follow the discipline of looking outward and avoid the trap and eventual defeat associated with an inside-out, we first perspective. The selling system needs to match how customers and clients make buying decisions whether they be transactional, consultative, or enterprise. These three buying modes are developed more fully in *Chapter Nine: Three Types of Sales, Three Ways to Create Value*.

OFFICERS

Officers report to generals and their focus is more tactical, as in taking that hill or this bunker. In the military they wear titles like lieutenant and their principal function is leading the troops in combat.

In business, the parallel function to officers would be managers to whom staff report on a day-to-day basis. In sales, the sales manager is the lieutenant who sets and guides the implementation of plans to win and retain specific accounts.

Tactical battle plans include:

1. Analyzing the decision makers and decision influencers. (See Chapter Fifteen on the Miller & Heiman (1998) model of economic, technical, user and coach influences).
2. Determining who from the selling team will cover the different decision makers and influences.
3. Identifying the decision criteria from the perspective of the buyer.
4. Determining how the buyer would evaluate each competitor on each criterion.

5. Setting a plan of action to establish the best competitive position in the eyes of the buyer.

Another crucial activity for sales managers is the monitoring of pipelines. They are at the core of a sales process (treated in Chapter Ten) and consist of a series of sales milestones that represent important and measurable steps to a major and complex sale.

Milestones vary from organization to organization. However, they have the common characteristic of motivating salespeople through a long sales cycle. They also enable sales managers to target the kind of coaching and help each salesperson needs. A salesperson who has difficulty moving from one early milestone to the next needs different kinds of help than one who has challenges with milestones later in the sales cycle.

SOLDIERS

Soldiers operate in the trenches and engage the enemy in the actual hand-to-hand combat of war. In business, the soldiers are the sales and customer service people who relate directly with clients and prospects and square off against the competition on a regular basis.

Sun Tzu writes that military leaders in ancient China would occasionally behead under-performing or cowardly soldiers to motivate the rest of the troops. Similarly, salespeople are occasionally fired as a reminder to others of the fatal consequences that could befall them.

In the previously cited film classic (Chapters One and Two) *Glengarry GlenRoss,* a poster titled *Sales Incentive Promotion* hangs behind Alec Baldwin's character Blake. It lists the prizes for that month's sales contest:

First prize: a Cadillac Eldorado
Second prize: a set of steak knives

To this list, Blake announces the third prize: *"You're fired!"*

More than any other business personnel, salespeople face the prospect of being fired. Almost always implicit, and sometimes just as explicit as Baldwin's portrayal in *Glenngarry GlennRoss,* salespeople know if they don't deliver in measurable terms, they face the prospect of termination. Dire consequences for under-performance are part of the lives of salespeople and soldiers alike.

Like soldiers, salespeople are trained and they develop individual approaches to combat. Modern day selling requires salespeople who know the

Table 7.1. Military positions, strategic scope, business positions, and strategic responsibilities.

Military Position	Strategic Scope	Business Position	Strategic Responsibilities
Sovereigns	Global, Identify Enemies and Allies	Directors, Shareholders	Broad Business Strategy Long-term Focus. Mission
Generals	Broad Military Strategy, Coordination of Land, Sea and Air Forces	CEOs, Presidents, VP for Sales, MDs	Strategic Planning SWOT Strategy Translation Market Segmentation
Officers	Specific Battle Plans	Sales Managers	Initial Value Propositions Identification of Milestones Departmental Pipeline Review
Soldiers	Hand-to-Hand Execution	Sales & Customer Service Representatives	Personal Pipeline Management Pre-call Planning Call Execution Call Follow-up

overall strategy and pursue their work within a replicable sales process. Reliance on mythological heroes who have god-given skills to make rain or close deals is not a strategy for success.

Comparisons between military and business positions and their respective roles in executing strategy are summarized in table 7.1.

Strategic selling requires synchronization at all four levels listed in table 7.1: shareholders, CEOs, sales managers, and the sales force. This is analogous to the different levels at which war is waged by Sovereigns, Generals, Officers, and Soldiers.

SCORECARD

1. Does your board help set strategic direction or does it get involved in day-to-day management?
2. Is your strategy conducted from an *outside-in* (customer-centered) or *inside-out* (product-centered) perspective?
3. Is your strategic planning coordinated at all four levels: directors, CEOs, sales managers and salespeople?

Chapter Eight

What Strategy Is and Isn't

Improving sales performance is at the pinnacle of the Strategy, Structure & People pyramid. It all starts there. And while we don't know any organization that does not conduct some kind of activity it calls strategic planning, does not mean they all do it well. In other words, just because you are doing something called planning, does not mean you can place a check mark next to it and turn your attention to your sales structure and process.

Below, we offer an analysis of how typical organizations approach planning and then contrast it to how high-performing organizations plan[1]. Which are you?

FOR TYPICAL ORGANIZATIONS STRATEGY IS:

An Event

True strategy is an ongoing and never ending process. Too many organizations and their leaders treat it as an event. It becomes one more thing, like the company Christmas party, that needs to get done each year.

An Off-site

Leaders like to go *off-site* to a nice facility swept away from the hassles of day-to-day management and reflect on the larger issues that face them, their organization, their industry, and the world. Often these functions are facilitated or led by a consultant who is effective at stimulating thought-provoking and interesting conversation about the future. Then they return feeling intellectually invigorated by the off-site.

Before too long, however, they are abruptly immersed into the everyday demands of returning phone calls and e-mails and putting out fires. Regrettably, the energy and good thinking done at the off-site rarely makes it back to the workplace.

A Document

Shelves and credenzas of executive offices are littered with strategic plans that get dusted off once a year – when it's time to prepare for the annual planning off-site. While documentation is useful for communicating and recording, too many organizations become over reliant on documents in the strategic planning process. The hazard is that conditions rapidly change, which can make positions captured in documents rapidly obsolete.

Done by Someone Else

While outside facilitation can be useful in planning, the organization needs to *own* the process. A sure sign of trouble is when an organization boasts about having its plan *done* by a brand name consulting firm.

Tasks Assigned to a Group

A certain way to kill a strategic initiative is to assign follow-up tasks to a group or committee. A group assignment diffuses accountability. Committee members will attend to tasks for which they are rewarded or subject to consequences if they go undone. Strategy initiatives assigned to a group are easy to dodge and likely to find their way to the back burner.

FOR HIGH-PERFORMING ORGANIZATIONS STRATEGY IS:

An Ongoing Process

Scanning the external horizon for both opportunities and threats is literally an everyday process. When a significant opportunity or threat is discerned, it should trigger internal adjustments. This process never ends.

Brief

While it is okay to have lengthy supporting documents that delve into issues like trends or competitive analysis, the essential elements of the plan need to be kept brief. The longer and more complicated the plan, the less likely it will be understood. Good plans are concise and easy to communicate and understand.

Action Oriented

If you cannot translate a plan into specific actions, it has little value. Good plans always have action items assigned to individuals or departments with accompanying deadlines.

Reviewed Regularly

If you are serious about strategic planning, the process will be reviewed at regular intervals. Again, strategy is not a document that gets opened on an annual basis. We find quarterly updates to the plan to be a fitting interval for most organizations. Ones that are managing urgent changes need to revisit their strategy more frequently.

Measurable

Wherever possible, strategic initiatives should be quantified. Statements, like *improve customer satisfaction,* are nothing but mush unless accompanied by some form of measurement. However, metrics should be kept simple, otherwise they can drain too much energy from the desired actions. Look for proxy indicators, like fewer returned items, as signs of customer satisfaction. While imperfect to professors and quants, proxy indicators serve well enough to inform you if your actions are achieving desired results. An approximate measure of what is important is always superior to a precise indicator of something that doesn't matter.

Translated Throughout the Organization

We routinely find that the only people in the organization who *know the plan* are the top-level executives. They operate under the mistaken notion that sending out a document or hosting a meeting on the strategic plan has adequately communicated it. While these are important steps, they are never enough. You know that a plan has been effectively translated when every person expected to take action knows what they are supposed to do differently, when they are supposed to do it, and what they are supposed to stop doing or do less.

Budget Driving

If we had a dime for every organization that has had a strategic initiative thwarted because the budget was already allocating resources to old initiatives, we would be wealthy men. The plan drives the budget. It is not the other way around.

SCORECARD

1. Do you treat strategic planning as an event or as an ongoing process?
2. If you do strategic planning as an off-site activity, does the momentum stay there or is there a sustained effort to have planning drive behaviors at the workplace?
3. When you hear *strategic plan*, is your first association to a document?
4. If someone else did the strategy, is there a sense that they own it?
5. Are follow-up activities pinned down to specific individuals with deadlines to meet?
6. Can the strategy be summarized succinctly?
7. Are there benchmarks against which strategy outcomes can be measured?
8. Does the plan drive the budget?

NOTES

1. Russell Brooks, formerly managing partner of R.P. Brooks & Associates, and currently CEO of SPE Federal Credit Union is the source for much of this chapter.

Chapter Nine

Three Ways to Create Value: Three Types of Sales

According to Hammer & Champy (2003), one of the keys to a business process is how tasks are carried out by different parts of an organization to create *customer value*. Further, we have emphasized that effective planning is conducted from an *outside–in*, or customer-centric perspective (Charan & Tichy 1998). An essential component of taking a systematic approach to selling then, is determining how your product or service creates value for your customer or client.

THE RACKHAM & DEVINCENTIS BUYER MODE MODEL

Rackham and DeVincentis (*Rethinking the Sales Force* 1999) assert that, when it comes to creating value for buyers, it is no longer one-size-fits-all. Indeed, they provide us with a model that outlines three selling strategies to create value determined by the mode in which the customer is functioning: transactional, consultative and enterprise. Understanding where your customer base functions in the Rackham & Devincentis model outlined below is essential to taking a systematic approach to selling.

Transactional Sales

Transactional purchases are made when the buyer already knows (or thinks he knows) everything he needs to know about the product or service. It is like buying a commodity, and time spent with a salesperson may not add value. In fact, it can even subtract value because commodity buyers resent wasting valuable time with someone asking them questions about what they already know and understand. Decisions to buy at this level are driven by the product, its price and ease of acquisition.

An allergy sufferer who has already had his ailment diagnosed by a physician, quickly recognizes the symptoms and knows that an antihistamine will dry up his runny nose. Operating from a transactional buying mode, he not only knows the symptoms, but the treatment that will correct it. Acquiring an antihistamine as quickly and reasonably as possible creates value. There is no need for expert consultation or expensive brands. Any product with an antihistamine will do, the faster the better.

The appropriate strategy for transactional level salespeople is to make the buying process as easy and headache-free as possible. Hard as it may seem, excellent consultative selling skills may be wasted on buyers who don't want or need a consultant. They just want the product fast and cheap.

Consultative Sales

At this level, buyers benefit from a salesperson helping them understand the full nature of their problem. This is the kind of setting where salespeople truly behave as consultants. They investigate to learn the nature and extent of the client's situation and related challenges. Then the consultative salesperson proposes customized solutions. Often, the trusting relationships skilled salespeople build become more important than the product or even the business that manufactures or represents it. Evidence of this is seen when clients follow salespeople as they move from one business to another.

Applying the aforementioned medical metaphor, let's consider a person with a new symptom: a growth on his shoulder. Concerned that it could be cancerous, he schedules a visit with a trusted physician. In this situation, the physician and his expertise in diagnosis are the keys to adding value. Contrasted to the buyer with the familiar runny nose who is shopping for a commodity, this symptom and its possible consequences are unknown, even feared. The physician's problem solving capabilities are more important considerations than price or ease of acquisition. Indeed, while price will drive the purchase of an antihistamine, it is rarely a factor when cancer treatments are being considered.

Good medical doctors do what good consultative salespeople should do. They start by diagnosing the problem by asking good questions and demonstrating empathic listening. Once the problem and its implications are thoroughly understood, solutions are proposed that the client could not do by himself. The key to successful consultative selling is building the relationship and winning the trust of the buyer.

Enterprise Sales

These are the rarest variety of sales and are made when sellers and buyers actually become partners. The focus of the enterprise sale is on the two organizations looking to create value neither one could accomplish alone. Business partners seek to leverage one another's competencies for mutual gain. The process is characterized by negotiations that start at the top and are typically carried out by cross-functioning work teams.

To play-out the medical metaphor, a partnership would unfold when a patient, who is an attorney by trade, negotiates a business alliance with her physician and attains a patent for a medical treatment the physician has discovered. Working together, they have leveraged their distinctive competencies for mutual gain.

Value creation at the enterprise level requires making the pie larger. It is more about shared gains for two enterprises than one party selling a product or service to another. Rather than being driven by salespeople, partnerships require negotiations that start at the top and have participation at multiple organizational levels.

Hybrid Sales

Yet a fourth buying mode has evolved as we have explored the Rackham & DeVincentis model with various clients. We call it the *hybrid* sale. While a purist might argue that it is not necessary, we have found that introducing the hybrid notion is helpful both in explaining the model and in reinforcing an essential point:

The same buyer can act in more than one mode simultaneously.

Hybrid buyers by definition are those that display characteristics of more than one buying mode. They may seek to purchase one product as a commodity when they are well informed on its benefits and know that it is not difficult to locate alternative suppliers. Yet for another product, they may have consultative needs and benefit from a skilled salesperson investigating their challenges and proposing customized solutions to their problems. Even at the enterprise level, a partner may have commodity or consultative buying needs. Even Microsoft buys paper clips.

There are some hybrid buyers who learn all they can during the early stages of a sale and then base their final decision on price. Life is not fair, and neither is the sales game.

PLAN BEFORE YOU ATTACK: SEGMENT MARKETS BY VALUE

According to Sawyer's translation (1994), a central theme of Sun Tzu's *The Art of War* is to do thorough planning and to formulate a comprehensive strategy prior to executing an attack.

The general who wins a battle makes many calculations in his temple before the battle is fought. The general who loses a battle makes but few calculations beforehand. Thus do many calculations lead to victory, and few calculations to defeat. (Sawyer 1994, 131)

Similarly, a systematic approach to selling requires many calculations, including a careful assessment of the mode through which the customer or client base is buying. Are they buying a commodity and seeking the best price and ease of acquisition? Or, do they only partially understand their problem and require expert consultation to arrive at a solution? Finally, are they seeking a partnership form of relationship to leverage unique competencies and make the pie in their market larger?

Rackham and DeVincentis (1999) invite us to rethink the knee-jerk reaction to market segmentation by customer size. The most typical segmenting scheme we encounter is to put customers into one of three buckets: big, medium, and small. Then, the most senior or skilled salespeople pursue customers in the biggest bucket, the next most skilled salespeople get the medium-sized bucket, and the newest and least skilled people are assigned to customers in the smallest bucket.

What is flawed with this most common of segmentation schemes, is that customers in the biggest bucket may be buying at the commodity level. They are experienced and believe they know their needs and range of solutions better than any salesperson. Rather than gaining benefit from a skilled consultative approach, they merely want a vendor to provide a rate sheet, preferably by mail. Anyone who has sold or tried to sell to a behemoth like Wal-Mart will tell you all they want from prospective vendors is to stand in line, make their pitch, and get out. Then, if you are a lucky enough to be a finalist, they beat you up on price and choose the lowest bidder (Anderson 2003).

Conversely, prospective buyers grouped in the smaller segments may need expert consultants to help them understand the problems, challenges, and opportunities in front of them. But rather than having a seasoned consultative pro managing this dialogue, they have been assigned a sales rookie who shows up at the call and throws up his rate sheet within the first minute. The prospective buyer is left without the crucial consulting and expertise they require in the buying process.

Follow the advice of Sun Tzu when it comes to segmenting your markets:

. . . one who knows the enemy and knows himself will not be endangered in a hundred engagements. One who does not know the enemy but knows himself will sometimes be victorious, sometimes meet with defeat. One who knows neither the enemy nor himself will invariably be defeated in every engagement. (Sawyer 1994, 179)

Perform your assessments for both sides, not just your own. Then, plan your attack according to how your prospect is buying, not just how big they are. Always remember that the key to winning sales is creating value for the buyer.

SCORECARD

1. Do you segment your markets by size, geography or buying mode (transactional, consultative, and enterprise)?
2. Do you emphasize value creation in selling?
3. Do you adapt value creation strategies by the three buying modes?

Chapter Ten

Process Driven Selling

Chapter Seven: Wage War-Win Business was dedicated to the four different levels at which war and business strategy are planned and waged. This chapter focuses on level three, corresponding to sales managers and the crucial work they do in developing specific strategies and tactics for those they lead. In selling, the single most important undertaking for a sales manager is to drive a process approach to guide his or her sales team in their efforts. Without an emphasis on process, salespeople will wander into battle like soldiers not knowing their terrain. As Sun Tzu observed:

> Configuration of terrain is an aid to the army. Analyzing the enemy, taking control of victory, estimating ravines . . . One who knows these and employs them in combat will certainly be victorious. One who does not know these or employ them in combat will certainly be defeated. (Sawyer 1994, 214)

Regrettably, it is not all that uncommon for us to encounter organizations where salespeople are left to figure out the selling terrain for themselves and, just as Sun Tzu proffers, are certainly defeated in combat. They are then terminated and new salespeople are recruited to replace them who, absent a process to follow, fare no better. It is not the soldier or salesperson who is to blame here. It is the sales manager's obligation to guide the troops under his or her command in the distinctive sales process that will lead to success. This begins with identifying the milestones in the sale process.

MILESTONES

Historically, milestones were stone markers set up along roadsides to indicate the distance to the next village. By reading milestones, travelers were able to judge how far they had come and how far it was to their next stop or ultimate destination. Milestones enabled travelers to plan their trip and calculate when lodging, food, water, and fuel would be available.

In selling, milestones indicate a sales team's current location in a long sales journey. Without a sense of milestones, salespeople wander about like lost travelers. They work just as hard as those with milestones to guide them, but it takes them much longer to arrive at the desired destination. Getting there often involves more luck than skill.

Conversely, a sales team with a process characterized by milestones knows what needs to be done next and by whom. Milestones keep sales teams on track, help them from wandering off course, and like they do for travelers, indicate how far the team has come, how far it needs to go, and perhaps most important, what it takes to get there. A milestone in the sales process is distinguished by two important criteria:

1. Importance

Each milestone must be important and represent significant progress in the underlying sales process toward a successful sale. The emphasis should be on achievement and results rather than mere activity. Having a chat with a client about the fortunes of a sports team is an activity that would not pass the importance test. To borrow again from the traveling metaphor, it is not about walking around for exercise or activity sake, it is about getting to a destination. It is also critical to recognize that there are no time limits defining the intervals between milestones in the sales process.

2. Measurability

There must be tangible evidence like receiving information, getting permission to make a proposal, or getting access to buyer influences. Salespeople do not satisfy the measurability requirement by just meeting and talking.

Milestones must meet both conditions if they are to be useful signposts for both salespeople and sales managers. Establishing credibility in the eyes of an *economic buyer*[1] is clearly important for a salesperson, especially in consultative selling. But how do you measure credibility? Creating a milestone around credibility is, thus, a formula for ambiguity. While the importance of a salesperson's credibility in the eyes of key decision influencers is beyond dispute, some kind of proxy is needed in order to measure it. For example, if credibility must precede proposal opportunity, then proposal opportunity, which can be measured (after all, it's either zero or one), becomes the milestone. If credibility with the *technical buyer*[1] is necessary before gaining access to the economic buyer, then access to the economic buyer becomes the milestone. In each of these examples credibility is the means to achieving the milestone.

Thus, if you're a sales manager and one of your salespeople tells you, "My next milestone with XYZ company is to establish personal credibility with the Chief Information Officer," ask him or her the following question: "If you are successful in establishing your credibility in the eyes of the Chief Information Officer, where will you be in the sales process?"

CREATING CUSTOMER VALUE

Setting steps to the selling process is not necessarily new. In fact, steps like *prospecting, qualifying, proposing &* and *closing* have been around for decades. The problem with them is that they are all about the sellers' activities and not about value creation for the customer or client. Recall that part of Hammer & Champy's (2003) definition of a business process or system (Chapter Nine) is the creation of value. To put it another way, the prospect-to-close steps represent a classic inside – out rather than an outside – in approach.

At the consultative level, milestones should be about creating value by uncovering performance-related problems and delivering solutions for the client, thereby demonstrating an outside – in approach. The metrics of milestones are indicators that the prospect or client is receiving value throughout the process by providing access to increasingly sensitive information and granting access to the full panel of decision influences.

DETERMINING MILESTONES

The best way to determine the milestones in the sales process is to examine the practices of the top performers. Chances are that there are some on your sales team who consistently demonstrate shorter sales cycles to winning the sale. They likely also have a higher yield of wins as they move from the beginning phases of the pipeline toward the latter stages. In other words, they are both more efficient with a shorter sales cycle and more effective by producing a higher yield.

In our experience, exemplary performers will have a process approach, whether they use that phrase or not. The key questions to ask pertain to the steps they follow in a typical successful sale. We find that focusing on a recent win and asking a top performer to walk through everything they did, start to finish, is a good way to structure the exemplary performer dialogue.

The next step is to look for common denominators among top performers. Chances are you will discover they are doing something the more typical performers are not. For example, we worked with a sales manager who learned that the exemplary performers on the team were arranging meetings between the technical influences on the client's buying team with their own technical specialists. They spoke a common language, and the technical specialists were able to win the trust of the buying team more readily than the salespeople. Coordinating meetings among technical steps was then *bottled* as a milestone, and performance increased across the entire team.

The key to this anecdote is that there was nothing mythical about what the exemplary performers were doing. They did not posses heroic traits like Paul Bunyan, nor were they natural born closers. Mere mortals were able to incorporate meetings among technical specialists into their individual systems and improve their performance. It is not about mythology. Rather, it is about a process driven approach with milestones that can be followed by everyone.

PIPELINE

Plotting all the milestones that characterize a sales process provides the outline of a *pipeline*. Salespeople then record all of their accounts, indicating where they fit with the various milestones. Effective management of the pipeline is one of the key aspects of both personal sales management and sales leadership, especially given the long lead times that are sometimes associated with major and complex deals. Pipelines are invaluable tools for the following:

Tracking

The pipeline report enables salespeople and their leaders to understand where action is taking place and where they need to redirect action (individually and on a group basis).

Forecasting

The pipeline report is an excellent predictor of future revenue. Over time, ratios can be determined on how much activity typically flows from one milestone to the next, and ultimately to new business.

Coaching

Once ratios have been reliably set, an individual's performance can be assessed against the team to help the manager pinpoint specific areas for coaching. For example, let's say the team's ratio is five formal presentations to two wins. If one team member is only winning one per five, he or she may need coaching or training in presentation skills.

Monitoring Strategy

The pipeline report can be used, not only to direct activities and techniques that might be focused on specific tactical situations, but also to help the sales manager monitor overall strategic direction for the group. For instance, if the aforementioned hypothetical sales team's *aggregate* ratio would drop from five presentations to two wins to five to one, it could be signaling a significant change in the market place.

Managing Resources

The pipeline report helps identify potential resource log jams and conflicts. As noted above, we once worked with a client with a milestone of arranging meetings with in-house and client-side technical specialists. A log jam occurred at that milestone. We learned that product specialists were not rewarded for assisting in sales conferences, just punished for falling behind with their internal assignments. It took a while to sort out the problem, but the pipeline report helped bring it to the surface.

TRANSACTIONAL VERSUS CONSULTATIVE PIPELEINES

The complexity of the consultative sales process derives from the multiple conditions of *fit* that must be satisfied before a sale can be made. In a transactional sale, there are usually only two fit conditions that must be met: ease of acquisition and price. In a consultative sale, however, the fit conditions are often more ambiguous due to the complex nature, both of the underlying problem or need and of the range of possible solutions. For example, while ease of acquisition and price are still conditions of fit in a consultative sale, the buyer tends to look at them differently compared to a transactional purchase decision.

From the consultative perspective, considerations of product fit extend to the buyer's perceptions of how well the seller has adapted or customized its proposed solution to address the need or opportunity and to the degree of creativity in the solution. The buyer will also consider whether the seller has demonstrated flexibility of thinking by being willing to work with the buyer in finding just the right product fit, even *after* the sale. These consid-

Table 10.1. **Examples of Rational and Relationship Decision Factors**

Rational Decision Factors	*Relationship Decision Factors*
Provider's Track Record	Provider's Flexibility of Thinking
Structure of the Solution	Customization of the Solution
Delivery / Implementation Timetable	How Well Provider Understands Us
Value Created (Compared to Cost)	Provider's Listening Skills
Documentation Requirements	Quality of Provider's Questions
System Compatibility	"Can We Work with Them?"

erations, in turn, influence the buyer's thinking about price (or, more accurately, about relative value). This is why buyers in a consultative mode are more willing to go with an offer that is not the cheapest; it just has to be priced fairly, given the buyer's perception of the value to be derived from the purchase.

When considering competing proposals in consultative purchase situations, buyers will often ask themselves questions such as: "Who do we think listened the best;" "Who asked the best questions along the way;" "Who seems to understand us the best;" and, ultimately, "Who do we think we can work with?" These questions reveal an important dimension to buyer decision-making on consultative sales: the relationship dimension. Whereas transactional purchase decisions are made on the basis of purely rational factors (product and price), consultative purchases involve a combination of rational and relationship factors. Research demonstrates that, the more complex the decision and the greater the consequences for the buyer of getting the decision right or wrong (in terms of the deal's ultimate success or failure), the more likely relationship factors will outweigh rational factors in the final choice of a provider. A key executive at one of the large North American investment banks illustrated this when he observed: "We [the investment banking community] give entirely too much credit to our clients for being able to differentiate among investment banks. They can't, at least not on any rational basis. Important mandate decisions are always made on the basis of relationship factors".

Examples of rational and relationship decision factors are listed in table 10.1.

REPERESENTATIVE CONSULTATIVE PIPELINE

A representative consultative pipeline is illustrated in figure 10.1. In this example, the pipeline has six milestone segments.

Milestone 1: Prospect Research & Initial Qualification

This is the research the salesperson is conducting before establishing initial contact with a prospective client.

Milestone 2: Access, Positioning & Discovery

Access can have both quantitative and qualitative dimensions. A salesperson may get in the door at a prospect organization (quantitative), but not be talking to the right thinkers or decision makers (qualitative). Positioning and investigating usually proceed in parallel, as the salesperson builds a performance-oriented knowledge base on the prospect (including *holistic understanding*[2] of their business), while at the same time seeking to influence how the key decision influencers perceive the *fit* between the capabilities, resources, and value potential of the salesperson's firm and the prospect's own goals.

Milestone 3: Preliminary Idea Discussion

Once the salesperson has reached a certain stage in his or her discovery process and has established a certain level of trust in the eyes of the key decision influences, he or she can become prescriptive. This is the stage in the sales process when the prospective client is ready to consider the salesperson's ideas. Or, as Seth Godin (1999) characterizes it, this is the stage where the prospective client raises his or her hand and says to the salesperson, "I give you permission to help me."

Milestone 4: Proposal Submittal

When preliminary ideas can be transformed into actionable proposals, it means the prospective client is prepared to take action if presented with the right solution. This is one of the most important milestones in the entire sales process.

Milestone 5: Final Negotiation

Consultative proposals usually require a period of nurturing, and possibly revision, before a client is ready to seriously negotiate a final deal. Once the final negotiations begin, the lead should be moved into Milestone Five in the pipeline.

Milestone 6: Commitment & Delivery

Once won, consultative sales still requires attention and, where necessary, internal collaboration and client handholding during the execution stage. In

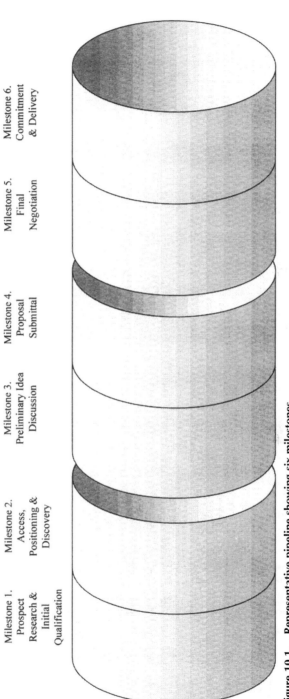

Figure 10.1. Representative pipeline showing six milestones.

order to ensure sufficient attention is paid to this key stage of the sales
process, all consultative pipelines should include Milestone that addresses
commitment and delivery.

Note that all six of these milestones are externally oriented. In some cases,
it may be necessary to include vital internal steps in the pipeline too. For example, getting internal approvals for offering product customization could be
a milestone in the pipeline.

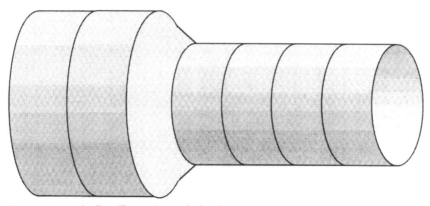

Figure 10.2.   Pipeline illustrating early log jams.

PIPELINE DIAGNOSIS

The shape of the pipeline can be used for diagnostic purposes as illustrated in
figures 10.2, 10.3 and 10.4.

If the pipeline takes the form of figure 10.2, it may be explained by:

- A new initiative
- New salespeople
- Skill deficiencies like initial qualification or conducting the investigation

If the pipeline takes the form of figure 10.3, it may be explained by:

- Possible internal collaboration issues
- Competition that becomes more intense at the middle stages of the sales
  process
- Morale issues because new prospects are not being loaded into the pipeline
- Skill deficiencies like proposal preparation and delivery

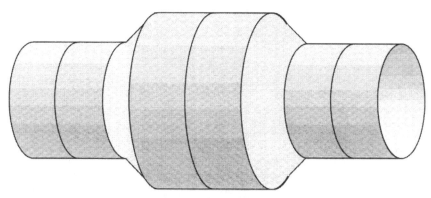

Figure 10.3.   Pipeline illustrating middle milestone log jams.

If the pipeline takes the form of figure 10.4 it may be explained by:

- A salesperson or sales team that has been totally absorbed by the final stages of the sales process and has neglected the earlier ones
- A salesperson, or salespersons, who expect to leave

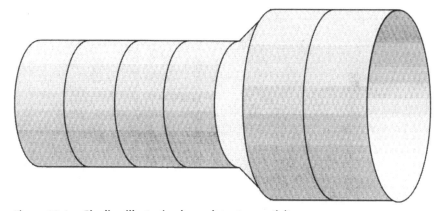

Figure 10.4.   Pipeline illustrating heavy late stage activity.

The pipeline is the single most valuable tool salespeople and their managers can possess. It will spell out with clarity what needs to be done next and by whom. It can also be use diagnostically to pinpoint problems and issues salespeople encounter advancing from one milestone to the next. There's no place to hide from a well-designed pipeline report.

3+3+ 3 BALANCE

Selling is a field where there is an emphasis on measurable performance. Consequently, salespeople often refer to their work as a *numbers game.* They are rewarded for *hitting their numbers,* and they are in line for consequences for missing them. We recently heard a sales leader for a Fortune 100 Company say to his team,

"Success here is easy. There are only three things you need to do. Know your number. Hit your number. Blow your number away."

With this emphasis on results, both salespeople and their managers have a tendency to focus on the later stages of the pipeline. We have worked with sales teams where the word pipeline has been synonymous with closes or wins. The hazard of focusing on the later stages of the pipeline is that success actually has more to do with earlier stage milestones, like prospecting for high probability buyers and *opening* the sales with skilled questioning and listening, which provide the feedstock for future revenues.

The best performers in sales maintain a balanced pipeline with prospects in the beginning, middle, and end phases. We emphasize balance with what we call the *3+3+3* routine as illustrated in figure 10.5.

To test for *3+3+3* balance, ask yourself these questions (alternatively, if you're a sales manager, ask a sales team member):

- What are the next three sales you expect to close?
- What are the next three proposals you expect to get out the door?
- What are the next three new contacts you expect to make?

Pipeline Milestones

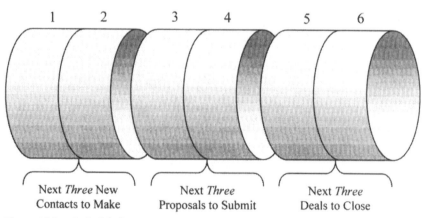

Figure 10.5.   3+3+3 balance.

Does this sound like transactional selling? It isn't. This exercise is all about maintaining a balanced focus across the entire pipeline. It is especially important in consultative selling, where long sales cycles often characterize the business and a *3+3+3* balanced pipeline is the key to a continuous sales flow.

SCORECARD

1. Do your milestones satisfy the dual criteria of:
   a. Importance?
   b. Measurability?
2. Have you placed your milestones in a pipeline?
3. Are you gathering data to establish ratios moving from one milestone to the next?
4. Have you conducted a pipeline diagnosis?
5. Have you checked your pipeline for 3+3+3 balance?

NOTES

1. The terms economic and technical buyer come from the Miller & Heiman model (1997) explained in more detail in Chapter Fifteen. Basically, the former is the final decision maker and the latter advices on technical considerations.

2. Holistic understanding is described in more detail in Chapter Fifteen under Know What, How & Why questioning.

Section Three

STRUCTURE

"I came to see, in my time at IBM, that culture isn't just one aspect of the game – it is the game."

Lou Gerstner

Chapter Eleven

Formal Structure

We often find organizations investing significant amounts of time and human resources in strategic planning. Typically, a not so cheap consultant facilitates the process. And while there are various ways to conduct the planning process, they usually have fairly standard elements. There is a view to the external environment and trends that could influence the industry. A competitive analysis is performed and new strategic initiatives are set.

Top-level executives come away from planning retreats excited about the strategic plan that will create the future for the firm. It gets communicated in a slick package throughout most of the organization. The analysis behind the strategy is both rigorous and detailed. In fact, the work is good. Everyone is sincere.

And then, nothing happens. Sound familiar? We see it all the time.

Having a brilliant strategy is never enough, if the structure is not in place to:

- Measure the right things
- Reward the right behaviors
- Provide consequences for the wrong behaviors
- Allocate resources to support the strategy

MEASURE THE RIGHT THINGS

The two cases described below illustrate structures that measured the *wrong things* and the results that accrued.

Case One

Increasing revenue was the highest strategic priority for this business. Everyone knows that there are two ways to accomplish this objective: retaining existing clients and winning new ones.

Sensing that they could improve on customer satisfaction, sales management engaged in a practice of periodically calling their client base and asking a series of questions to determine how satisfied they were with the service they were receiving from the account managers assigned to them. They would ask how frequently the account manager saw them, how much time was spent with them, and the like. Results were drawn up and posted for each account and each account manager. Incremental improvements on these measures were cited and large ones celebrated.

Simultaneously, the same account managers were expected to call on new prospects. However, the tracking here was not as rigorous, and comparisons of how one account manager was doing against the rest of the pack were not made, at least not publicly.

Want to guess which of the two initiatives received more attention from the account managers? Was it with existing clients where their behavior was measured and publicly compared to others? Or, was it for new prospects where the tracking was less painstaking and there were no public performance comparisons? The answer is obvious.

Case Two

This investment bank, like many in that industry, began tracking the number of pitches made by each banker on a weekly basis (figures usually cover both the week past and the week ahead). These figures are studied by the senior leadership of the firm, not just by the heads of coverage groups. While the leading individual performance indicators are tied to revenue and collaboration, the pitch-tracking system has led to a natural reaction on the part of the bankers: make sure you don't look bad in the weekly pitch statistics. This, in turn, has contributed to a phenomenon on the client side that many buyers now refer to as *pitch fatigue*: clients growing tired of a seemingly endless schedule of investment bankers coming through their offices making ill-prepared, unfocused pitches. The result is that many of these same prospects are now much more restrictive about granting bankers' requests for meetings. As one potential buyer pleaded in a recent research interview, "They [investment bankers] just don't seem to get it. Their systems seem to generate hundreds of pitch books that lead, in turn, to hundreds of dead end meetings."

These serve as perfect illustrations of what we repeatedly find. You get what you measure. The business in case one got a sales team that gave a lot of attention to existing accounts (what they were measuring), while doing little to win new business. The investment bank in case two succeeded in annoying its prospects and thereby made it more difficult to secure meetings.

Before a strategy can succeed, existing metrics need to be examined to ensure that you are counting the right things. Too often, we find a strategy that requires new behaviors with a structure stuck measuring the old ones.

It is never enough to tell a sales team what the new strategy is and what new behaviors are expected of them. You also need to outline the how and what of the new metric system. As Lou Gerstner found at IBM, "People don't do what you expect but what you inspect." (2002, 211).

DIFFERENT METRICS FOR DIFFERENT KINDS OF SALES

The Rackham & DeVincentis (1999) buyer mode model developed and introduced in *Chapter Nine: Three Types of Sales, Three Ways to Create Value* is crucial to setting up measurements for the sales structure. The metrics of transactional and consultative sales are quite different. In the transactional mode it is appropriate and fitting to measure indicators of how hard salespeople are working. Neil Rackham (1991, 14) refers to this as sales efficiency, or getting in front of the right prospects and clients for the right amounts of time in a cost sensitive manner. Recall that the transactional level buyer already knows about the product and is looking for a good price and easy acquisition. Time spent acting as a consultant to solve problems does not necessarily add value for a commodity buyer.

Transactional metrics include:

- Activity reports
- Numbers of new contacts made
- Numbers of sales calls completed
- Short term sales volumes

However, when your buyers are operating from a consultative mode, a different set of metrics is required. It is here that many organizations make a classic error. While giving lip service to consultative selling, they continue to monitor metrics that fit the transactional mode. For example, one of our clients, a major financial services firm, went through an agonizingly long market segmentation process. Their concern was that salespeople were spending too much time with smaller accounts and not enough with the larger, key accounts. In an effort to redirect the focus of the sales team, they prescribed monthly targets for the number of calls for each market segment. For example, the sales team was expected to meet with large accounts twice a month, mid-size clients once a month, and smaller prospects and clients just once a quarter.

This kind of structure would be fine in a commodity buying system. However, their large clients were operating from a true consultative mode and were in need of a relatively complex solution. Rather than adding value with frequent meetings, salespeople were becoming a nuisance to their most important customers.

The key metrics for consultative level sales have to do with working smart, or what Rackham (1991, 14) refers to as sales effectiveness. In this buying mode, value is added when salespeople earn the trust of their clients in crafting solutions to their problems. Measuring consultative considerations like *trust* and *crafting solutions* is obviously harder than tangible kinds of behaviors. Nonetheless, if you take the easy way out and count what's tangible, you will be making a serious mistake because you will always get what you inspect not what you expect. In consultative selling a proxy or approximate metric is more effective than a hard and precise activity metric.

The surest way to construct a set of good consultative metrics is to have a well developed pipeline in place, as prescribed in the preceding chapter. Recall that the dual criteria of milestones in the pipeline are that they are: 1. important and 2. measurable.

Representative consultative metrics include:

- Prospect research and initial qualification
- Access and investigation
- Preliminary idea discussion
- Proposal submittal
- Final negotiation
- Commitment and delivery

CRITERIA FOR METRICS

We find a fascination, particularly among sales teams, with reward systems. Some invest a king's ransom in their design and development. Our view is that having the right metrics in place always precedes the doling out of rewards. A good set of metrics satisfies the following criteria:

Simplicity

Gathering data takes time. Salespeople are busy. Make metrics that are as simple and streamlined as possible. Avoid the temptation of thinking a complicated and intellectually challenging set of metrics will lead to better results. It won't. If it gets too complicated salespeople won't understand it or care.

Important to Salespeople

If the metrics add value to the work salespeople do, they will continue to use them. If they appear bogus and distracting, salespeople will fake the data. It is not at all uncommon for salespeople to complete weeks of activity reports, one sitting at a time, and enter just enough data keep the sales manager away. A good way to ensure what you are measuring is indeed important to salespeople is to involve them in the development of milestones. Since measurability is one of the criteria for a milestone, metrics are a natural byproduct of this exercise.

Match the System

As noted above, transactional and consultative sales are characterized by different systems. They should have different metrics as well. Since the metrics of the commodity sale are clear and obvious, they are too often applied to consultative selling where they can be counterproductive. Because you can get an exact reading on activity, like the number of calls made, does not mean that you are measuring the right kind of behavior. In consultative selling, where the emphasis is on working smart, using a simple commodity metric means you are not.

Accommodate Individual Styles

Counting the number of putts a golfer requires in a round would be an appropriate metric for that sport. But we shouldn't care if the player uses a claw grip like Chris DiMarco or a traditional grip like Tiger Woods. Putting is a matter of individual style. So are many sales activities. We should focus on the information a salesperson can gather during an investigation and not try to script everyone with the same questions. In other words, metrics should focus on results like putts made and information gathered rather than individual styles of putting or asking questions.

REWARDS

The Watergate investigative reporters Woodward and Bernstein made famous the saying, *"Follow the money"*. However, the axiom for anyone who wants to understand why people behave the way they do in organizations is to: *Follow the rewards*. But it is not quite as simple as the trail Woodward and Bernstein pursued to crack Watergate, because there are two kinds of rewards: extrinsic and intrinsic.

Extrinsic rewards are the carrots at the end of the stick. They are always provided by someone else, tangible, and usually bankable.

Intrinsic Rewards, on the other hand, come from within and are intangible. They have to do with a sense of accomplishment, pride associated with doing a good job, learning, growing, a sense of mastery and belonging. While it is less common for managers to consider intrinsic rewards, they are often more powerful than the extrinsic variety. As Sun Tzu said:

> Unhappy is the fate of one who tries to win his battles and succeed in his attacks without cultivating the spirit of enterprise; for the result is waste of time and general stagnation. (Sawyer 1994, 198)

Research shows that extrinsic rewards can influence performance only when management needs more of something or needs it faster. As Alfie Kohn (1993) observes in *Punished by Rewards*, pay and performance are not related in intellectual or complex kinds of tasks. Thinkers like Kohn and Rackham cause us to question the effectiveness of extrinsic rewards in higher level consultative selling characterized by long sales cycles and where success is more a function of working smart.

DIFFERENT REWARDS FOR DIFFERENT KINDS OF SALES

Many organizations make the same mistake with their reward systems that they do when setting up their metrics: They employ the kinds of rewards that work at the transactional level to consultative sales. For transactional buyers, the sales cycle is typically short and buyers are principally interested in two considerations: price and ease of acquisition. Extrinsic rewards for transactional level sales can be effective because doing *more* and doing it *faster* directly determine performance. When selling a commodity, the formula for success is simple: more calls = more sales.

Consultative selling, however, requires vastly different strategies than the commodity variety. At this level, sales cycles typically last months, even years. Handing out goodies for working harder or faster has little impact on shaping behaviors that lead to trusting relationships, the key to consultative level success.

Motivation needs to be sustained over the long haul, and it is far trickier than rewarding the kinds of behaviors that are effective for transactional sales. Milestones are essential because the achievement of each, if you will, mini-sale needs to be rewarded. For example, completing a comprehensive buyer profile requires asking good questions that are followed by empathic listening. It is a crucial step to the ultimate objective of winning the account, which may still be many months away. It needs to be rewarded intrinsically.

INTRINSIC REWARDS BEST PRACTICES

Sales leaders who are exemplary at using intrinsic rewards ensure that the rewards:

1. Fit the culture and 2. Are customized to the receiver. A practice of legendary football coach Vince Lombardi described in *When Pride Still Mattered* (Maraniss 1999) illustrates point number one. Lombardi and his staff would breakdown the performance of every player on every play. Performance would be graded as a zero, one, or two. Lombardi would then conduct an *awards ceremony* when he honored high performers by calling them to the front of the room where he handed out crisp five or ten dollar bills. Honorees felt considerable pride. Players with zeros on their report cards dreaded the pending film analysis.

This practice used intrinsic rewards to build pride in people executing the right skills on every play. The reward system was a powerful one because it fit the culture. What mattered was what the ceremony represented: being recognized for doing an excellent job by your boss in front of your peers. The money was secondary. Tight end Gary Knafelc said, "It was amazing how prideful you would become . . . It could have been five thousand dollars it meant so much." (Maraniss 1999, 376).

Guard Jerry Kramer once joked, "Lombardi treated us all the same, like dogs." It's a funny line that wasn't true. (The part about being treated the same, anyway.) Lombardi knew that players like Paul Hornung didn't mind being taken to task during practice. Others like Willie Davis and Fuzzy Thurston couldn't stand being singled out. Accordingly, he would blast Hornung anytime he screwed-up (usually for being late for curfews) and talk privately with Davis and Thurston. Quarterback Bart Starr was one of those who preferred private conversations. He approached Lombardi and told him he felt his leadership effectiveness was undermined whenever he got his butt chewed at practice. From then on, Lombardi held his tongue and reserved all of his concerns for private quarterback-to-coach talks. Starr's performance took off, and the Packers started to win. Lombardi customized his approach to fit each player, illustrating point number two: effective intrinsic rewards need to be customized for the receiver. Winning teams, whether in football or sales, are led by people who recognize the power of intrinsic rewards.

REWARD THE RIGHT BEHAVIORS

For national sales teams, it is fairly common to have coverage plans calling upon the same account managers to service both regional accounts and major national ones. More than once, we have uncovered flawed structures where account managers were rewarded more for attending to the smaller regional accounts while giving less attention to the national customers accountable for most of the revenue.

Why? Well, the account managers were reporting to regional, not national sales managers. The regional managers drove, rewarded, and emphasized regional performance and that is what they got. The structure was not set up to reward the right behaviors, those that focused on cultivating relationships with national accounts.

Strategy comes first. Then, the structure needs to be in place to reinforce and reward the right behaviors. While these clients named a strategy of increasing sales from national accounts, no amount of smart tactics or excellent skills would bring about those revenue targets without a change in structure.

CONSEQUENCES

The king once put Sun Tzu's skill at military strategy to a test. To answer, Sun Tzu had two of the king's favorite concubines lead simulated companies comprised of palace women. Sun Tzu instructed the companies to "advance, withdraw, go left or right or turn around" in accordance with a drumbeat. (Sawyer 1994, 80-81). However, at the sound of the drum, rather than advancing, withdrawing, or turning as instructed, the pretend soldiers covered their mouths with their hands and laughed.

In response, Sun Tzu summoned the executioners axe and, in accordance with the code of military discipline, had the two company commanders beheaded. When the drum was beat the next time, the two companies advanced, withdrew, and turned in perfect unison without a single snicker.

While we come up a little short of advocating the execution of salespeople who giggle at staff meetings, there is no denying that consequences for not following instructions can be attention-getting and play a role in shaping human behavior. Further, it is a dimension of sales force management that often goes neglected.

New strategy typically requires salespeople to demonstrate a new behavior and cease an old one. For example, let's say the sales team has been asked to involve technical people in the sales process. Sales managers expect them to identify different buyer influences in an account and align technical experts on the client side with technical people on the internal team. What happens if they don't?

Or, you have introduced a new team-based pipeline system that requires each team member to report on his individual pipeline activity. What happens if one or more salespeople don't?

We know the answer to these questions and so do you. Others on the sales team will look at one another and ask, why bother? Before long, both initiatives, involving technical staff in the sales process and developing a team-based pipeline, are finished.

It is human nature to want to hand out awards to top selling salespeople and avoid rendering consequences when they blow off an expectation. But, don't let it happen. It will prove toxic to the success of any project that requires salespeople to start doing something new or to cease doing something old.

ALLOCATE RESOURCES TO SUPPORT THE STRATEGY

Sun Tzu said, ". . . the victorious army is like a ton compared with an ounce while the defeated army is like an ounce weighed against a ton." (Sawyer 1994, 184). Regrettably, many sales forces are stuck waging their battles with the equivalent of ounces, instead of the tons of resources they require. Often this is due to a phenomenon we refer to as *the tyranny of the budget process*. It goes like this.

A smart outside-in strategy is in place. We know not just ourselves, but also have a good understanding of how our clients are buying. The metrics and reward structures are in place to measure and then reward the right kinds of behaviors. Thinking we are all set to do battle, we discover that the resources we need to be victorious are already committed to an out-of-date strategy imbedded in last year's budget.

Most organizations simply acquiesce to this form of bureaucratic oppression by postponing the implementation of a new strategy until a new budget can support it. Often the strategic opportunities have closed by the time the next budget cycle rolls around. It becomes one of those Catch 22 phenomena where you can't allocate resources for a strategy until it is too late to matter.

There is only one way to overcome the tyranny of the budget process: put strategy in position to drive the budget. Now, this is easier said than done. It sometimes requires a cultural upheaval and prevailing over the budget mavens who believe their place in heaven will be incrementally jeopardized by every dollar that is over budget or not listed in a column with an existing budget heading.

There is not much art to transforming the historic budget-first culture to a strategy that drives the budget organization. Usually it just takes brute strength and an understanding board. Making the transition can be ugly, but rest assured, while you are sitting on a smart strategy until the budget can support it, your competitors who put strategy ahead of budget will be out eating your lunch. If you are serious about winning a sales battle, equip your foot soldiers with the equivalent of tons of resources, not ounces.

MARKET SEGMENTATION & ORGANIZATION CHARTS

Speaking of structure, two topics that are found in different chapters could as well find a home here. The first, market segmentation is treated in Chapter Nine in the strategy section. It was simply necessary to introduce the concepts of segmenting markets by value rather than size as an essential step in planning strategy. The second, organization charts, is addressed in the following chapter when we compare a representative formal organizational chart to what an informal one looks like.

SCORECARD

1. Do you employ different metrics to track different kinds of sales, transactional and consultative?
2. Are your metrics:
   a. Simple?
   b. Important to the sales team?
3. Do your metrics:
   a. Match your sales system?
   b. Accommodate individual styles?
4. Do you use a mix of both extrinsic and intrinsic rewards?
5. When necessary, do you render consequences in a timely fashion?
6. Do you suffer from the tyranny of the budget, or are resources allocated to support the budget?

Chapter Twelve

Informal Structure

Every organization functions on two levels: the formal and the informal. The formal structure is the easy one to see and understand. It is outlined in organization charts and job descriptions, and monitored by performance reviews and the like.

On the other hand, the informal structure, sometimes called the culture, is usually invisible or at least difficult to make out, particularly for newcomers and visitors. But beware of the fatal trap of ignoring it. Although hard to discern, the informal structure can be a powerful force that needs to be negotiated in every organization for every initiative, including instituting a systematic approach to selling.

Just ask Lou Gerstner, retired CEO of IBM. He addresses issues of informal structure and culture in his *Who Says Elephants Can't Dance (2002)*. He came to learn that at IBM, the culture had become *the* elephant. IBM was big and slow moving, focused inwardly on its mainframes in a market that required responsiveness and customer focus. The key to Gerstner's success was analogous to getting an elephant to dance. "I came to see, in my time at IBM, that culture isn't just one aspect of the game – it is the game." (Gerstner 2002, 182)

Gerstner learned that navigating the informal structure can be every bit, and sometimes even more, important to a leaders' success, as managing the formal one. If it is not written down anywhere, and is indeed invisible, how does a sales leader come to learn the aspects and dimensions of the informal organization?

The remainder of this chapter is dedicated to two methods to advance your understanding of the informal organization. The first is to examine your formal organization chart for clarity. Sales organizations are notorious for having fuzzy reporting relationships occupied by people whose titles bear little to no relationship to their actual responsibilities. It is not uncommon, for example, for senior level salespeople to wear the label *manager* in their title, even when they manage no one other than themselves. Sometimes lofty job titles are assigned to junior level people in the belief that the titles will impress prospects and clients.

The second method for gaining insight into the informal structure is to explore the terms of the psychological contract. Every organization has them and the terms usually exert more influence over performance than those in the formal contract.

ORGANIZATION CHARTS: BE WARY OF DOTTED LINES

We all know what organization charts look like. Software is readily available to make them easy to graph. Everyone in the organization, or at least his or her job title, is charted in a little box with a line connecting it to the person to whom that person reports. Sometimes the charts get a little untidy, with dotted lines going to other boxes or lines making horizontal rather than vertical connections. The formal organization chart is always a good place to start to get a sense of how influential the informal structure is in an organization. They follow this axiom:

The more horizontal lines you find in an organization chart, and particularly the more dotted lines you discover, the more influential the informal structure.

Horizontal and dotted lines dilute the authority of the formal structure and the influence of the person occupying a box with an incoming vertical line. Thus, a formal organization structure that looks like the one depicted in figure 12.1 has most, but not all, of its energy operating at the formal level.

On the other hand, the chart illustrated in figure 12.2 suggests an organization where most of its energy is siphoned off into the informal structure. What is represented below is a compilation of many ill-conceived sales organization charts we have seen.

If your organization chart looks like a variation of the one in figure 12.2, it's safe to say that no one really knows who reports to whom. Your first consideration should be pulling out the latest version of your curriculum vitae with an eye toward updating it. If, however, you are a leader with influence, you should bite the bullet and make structural changes, because this kind of structure will always lead to sub-optimal performance.

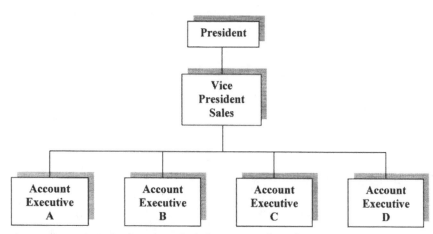

Figure 12.1.   Organization chart depicting a strong formal structure

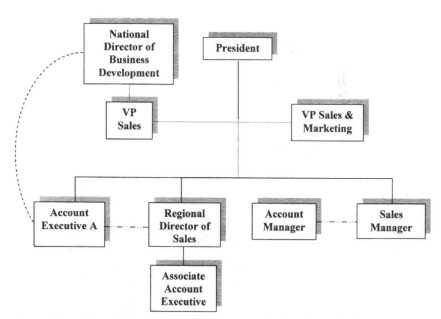

Figure 12.2.   Organization chart depicting a strong informal organization

ORGANIZATION CHARTS:
SYMPTOMS OF ORGANIZATIONAL HEALTH

People who inhabit a structure characterized by lots of dotted and horizontal lines may work just as hard, indeed probably harder, than those in an efficient structure. However, political maneuvering and backside covering absorb much of their effort.

Organizations are much like people. And, just like people, organizations operate at various stages of health. Indeed, theorist Wilfred Bion (1961) advanced a model applying psychoanalytic principles to understanding groups and organizations. Like people, he proffered, organizations have a finite amount of energy to invest. A person who is unhealthy emotionally will need to devote most of his energy into coping with his psychological problems. An obsessive compulsive who washes her hands thousands of times a day does little work.

Similarly, an unhealthy organization puts most of its energy into the political activities that support the informal structure. Thus, while the formal agenda may call for focusing on external objectives like customer focus and value creation, an unhealthy organization will expend its energy on internal issues. Instead of obsessive hand washing, people in an unhealthy organization will spend their energy positioning for titles, power, and the prestige that goes with office assignments and administrative assistants. It is not that the convoluted organization chart illustrated in figure 12.2 is the cause of unhealthy organizational behavior. But it is a symptom.

CO-OPTING INFORMAL LEADERS

Even the healthiest organization has some energy flowing into the informal structure, and instituting a systematic approach to selling will require attention to its leaders. A good approach is to try to chart the informal structure by answering the question of who wields power and influence in the informal structure.

For example, we once worked with a client where most of the salespeople were in their late twenties and early thirties. The sales leaders were in their forties. However, there were two senior account executives in their fifties. They would take the younger sales talent under their wings and mentor them.

Over time, they became the leaders of the informal structure. Whenever the formal leaders would announce an initiative, members of the sales team would look to the two senior members for their interpretation. "Is this something we need to take seriously or can we ignore it?" they would ask. With the power of Roman Emperors over the life of the initiative, the more senior account executives would sit back and offer either the thumbs up or thumbs down sign. The initiative would live or die accordingly.

Your organization has informal leaders as well. The best strategy for dealing with them is to co-opt them and make them part of the leadership effort on an informal basis. Our sales leaders in the above case followed this tack and started inviting the views of the senior account executives *before* they would formally announce an initiative to the full team. Flattered to be involved in a way that recognized their seniority, the senior account executives began to support rather than fight the plan.

THE PSYCHOLOGICAL CONTRACT

Every organization executes a formal contract with its employees. The terms list the responsibilities to be performed by the employee in exchange for compensation and the benefits to be paid by the organization. Like organization charts and job descriptions, formal contracts are artifacts of the formal organization.

However, another agreement is also at play in the informal organization. This one is neither signed nor dated. You cannot find it on file in the HR office, nor are they reviewed by legal counsel. Nonetheless, these understandings are real and can exert a powerful influence on how people perform and produce. They are the psychological contracts each and every person holds with his or her employer.

Sometimes the terms of the psychological contract are at odds with the formal positions stated by the organization. For instance, we have several clients who espouse their commitments to managing workloads to ensure work-life balance for staff. While this is a formal assertion, staff are quick to observe who gets promotions and discern that the people winning them are those working evenings and weekends. The terms of the psychological contract are clear. Those who work the longest hours are those who get promoted, not those managing balanced lives.

According to writers like Conway & Briner (2005) the term psychological contract has been around since the 1960s, although precise references to it are hard to find. Generally speaking, the psychological contract has to do with perceived promises and obligations the employee believes are owed.

Put more simply, the terms of the psychological contract are, *If I do this, I get that* as listed in table 12.1.

If the terms of the psychological contract are breached, look out. We have observed countless situations where leaders are left clueless because a

Table 12.1.   Terms of a psychological contract.

If I . . .	I get . . .
do the most work . . .	promoted
do the most work	the biggest raise or bonus
hit my numbers . . .	job security
agree with my boss	job security
have been here the longest . . .	promoted.
have been here the longest . . .	job security
work hard . . .	a pat on the back.
have been here the longest . . .	the best accounts
win a big deal	credit

salesperson, or sometimes an entire team, has stopped performing for no apparent reason. The answer often can be found in the perception that a promise imbedded in the psychological contract had been broken.

Here's an example. One of our client's star performers literally shut down. Instead of actively making calls and conducting face-to-face client meetings, he was sulking around the office listlessly passing time. His sales manager chalked-up the first few days of this behavior as just an aberration, likely caused by some personal problems.

Finally, the sales leader invited his sullen star into his office for a chat. What he got was entirely unexpected: a red-faced explosion about how he (the sales manager) had stolen credit for the star's recent win by listing it as a top departmental achievement in a report.

That the sales manager never intended to take personal credit for the win did not matter. The perception the star held was that the terms of his psychological contract had been broken. *When I win a big deal, I get credit.*

It is important to note that in the case described above, the terms of the formal contract were followed precisely, in that a generous bonus for the win was calculated and added to the star's paycheck. What led to his undoing was a perception that an implicit promise had been violated.

Another important lesson to be derived here is that it is much easier to honor the terms of the psychological contract than it is to repair a breach after it happens. It took a long time for the sales manager, who was well intended all along, to regain the trust and eventually the performance of his star salesperson.

Do you know the terms of the psychological contract for your organization? If you do, you will be able to do the following exercise filling in both sides of the *If I do . . . I get* table below.

Take a tip from Lou Gerstner and our sales manager client. Influencing sales performance requires as much, if not more, attention to what is going on

If I do	*I get . . .*

in the informal organization as the formal one. Second, know and manage the terms of the psychological contract. If they are breached, performance will suffer greatly.

SCORECARD

1. Could you explain your organizational chart to a busy bartender?
2. Is your organizational chart cluttered with horizontal or dotted lines?
3. Do you co-opt informal leaders to gain their support when introducing important initiatives?
4. Can you list the terms of the psychological contract at your organization?
5. Do you give as much attention to managing the informal organization as the formal one?

Section Four

PEOPLE

"Of all the decisions an executive makes, none is as important as the decisions about people because they determine the performance capacity of the organization."

Peter Drucker

Chapter Thirteen

Recruit for Talent

Back in Chapter Two, we refer to the sign displayed over the sales manager's office door, while Alec Baldwin's Blake lays into the sales force in the film classic *Glengarry GlenRoss*. Once again, it reads:

Salesmen are born. Not made.

This is the core of the Rainmaker myth, and many otherwise smart and competent companies subscribe to it. They simply look to recruit, select, or assign people with what they believe to be natural, god-given gifts to make it rain (read: bring in business). If we could assign a sales myth debunking squad to replace that sign, they would hang one that would read:

Sales performance requires talents and skills.

While it may not win a bumper sticker slogan contest, it is indeed the prescription for optimizing sales performance. If we were in the basketball business, we would seek to assemble a team of players that had *both* talents and skills. For the former, we would search for natural gifts like speed, height, and jumping ability. Regarding the latter, we would consider skills that can be learned like dribbling, passing, and shooting.

DEFINITIONS OF TALENTS AND SKILLS

Talents

The definition of a talent then, is a trait that we either have or don't have. Strictly speaking, talents are an accident of birth. While a basketball coach may work with her players to do weight training to run faster or jump higher, there will be only marginal impact. Fundamentally, some of us can run fast and jump high, while others of us can't.

Skills

On the other hand, skills can be taught and learned. With enough practice, anybody can learn to dribble, pass, and shoot a basketball. Similarly, anyone who works in a modern office can learn the skills of getting and sending electronic mail and using computer software like word processing and spreadsheets.

To continue with the basketball metaphor, it should be obvious that the best teams have players with both talents and skills. Lisa Leslie, the star center of the LA Sparks, has terrific low post skills. She also has the talents (height and jumping ability) to be the only player in the league who has dunked during a game. With a roster of players combining talents and skills, the Sparks are two time WNBA champions.

Like basketball, selling requires both talents and skills to win. But, unlike basketball, there is far less consensus on what comprises the fundamental talents and skills for selling success. Recruiting, like selling, requires a systematic approach. The remainder of this chapter will be dedicated to providing a roadmap for a systematic approach to recruiting sales talent.

BREAKING THE RULES OF MANAGEMENT

Many best selling business books are bunk, based on one guy's opinion or written by a celebrity coach appealing to the prominent male fantasy that life is nothing more than a metaphor for sport. Occasionally, there are exceptions, like Neil Rackham's (1988, 1991 & 1999) research-based contributions on selling and sales management. *First Break All the Rules* (1999), written by two researchers from the Gallup Organization (Marcus Buckingham and Curt Coffman), is yet another. It is based on a twenty-five year study of millions of surveys that sought to isolate common practices of effective managers.

The title is not only catchy, it also speaks to the central message of the book: conventional rules of management don't work. For example, Buckingham and Coffman found that great managers don't look for *skills* derived from years of experience in a like kind of position when recruiting. Rather, they focus on natural *talents,* and coach and teach the necessary skills after selection.

I KNOW IT WHEN I SEE IT. NO YOU DON'T

Years after the publication of *First Break All the Rules,* we still find most sales recruiting efforts focusing on experience and the skills it builds rather than on natural talents. Some are driven by the fear that a hungry competitor will swoop into a vacant territory and steal away existing business. Rather than recruiting for talent, businesses will instead seek someone with industry knowledge who can plug the hole as quickly as possible. Other sales executives pass a vacancy off to the HR department as one more annoyance that is just a part of day-to-day management. HR then advertises for industry experience and strong closing skills. Managers follow up by putting the finalists through some form of beauty contest with modified versions of swimsuit, evening gown, and congeniality criteria. Of course, they conclude the contest with their own versions of questions like, "If you had the power to end world hunger or war, which one would you choose and why?"

"What do you look for?" is a question we like to ask managers involved in filling a sales position. Some have told us they judge a candidate by how fast he or she walks because they believe foot speed to be an indication of drive. (Beware, the slow moving candidate suffering an ankle sprain from a weekend softball game. You don't have a prayer with that interviewer.)

Others will make the association that selling requires enthusiasm and that the candidate who shows the most energy during the interview will surely be the most enthusiastic on a sales call. (Ever hear of faking?) Still others will say that they look for an existing book of business, assuming that, if the candidate could do it before, he or she can do it again. (What if a talented salesperson got assigned a real dog of a territory?)

Most of our clients will confess that when selecting sales talent, it is just an *intuitive* or *gut feeling.* They will affirm this approach by professing that, simply put: *They know it when they see it.* Our response, equally simple, is: *No you don't.*

Selecting winning sales talent is too important to be left to guess work or gut feelings. It requires a methodical approach that follows the sales system. While the Supreme Court ruled that we may know pornography when we see it, we cannot identify sales talent without a system.

TALENTS & SKILS FOLLOW THE SYSTEM

The kinds of talents and skills required to be successful are determined by the sales system and the nature of the sale that characterizes it. This is analogous to college coaches recruiting and building skills that fit the system they use.

If you have a run-oriented offense, like Nebraska, you'll seek linemen who can pull and block downfield. On the other hand, if your offense is pass-oriented, like Florida, you will want talented passing quarterbacks, fleet receivers, and linemen skilled at pass blocking.

Recruiting and training follows the system in sales, as well. If your customers are buying from a transactional mode, you require a sales team that can knock on a lot of doors in an efficient fashion and remain optimistic that the next call they make will result in a sale. They need to represent products that are easy to acquire and offered at a good price. The emphasis here is on working hard, and the value created for the buyer is intrinsic to the product.

If, on the other hand, your clients are buying consultatively, you want a sales team able to earn the trust of prospects and clients and skilled at diagnosing problems and customizing solutions. They should be able to ask good questions, listen, and help clients and prospects understand the depth of their problems. Acting as consultants from the same side of the desk, they then offer solutions to the problems they have uncovered. Hard work is always important, but at the consultative level, the emphasis is on working smart. Value is added through the consultative process, and the product is less important than the trusting relationship established between the client and the consultative salesperson.

Enterprise selling is the most uncommon variety and typically negotiated at the highest level of the organization. In enterprise selling, it is not a product (transactional level) or a solution (consultative level) but the entire enterprise that creates value. Enterprise level salespeople need to be senior and experienced in business analysis and strategy. They require skills to coordinate cross-functioning teams and to be able to negotiate at the highest level.

KNOW WHAT YOU'RE LOOKING FOR BEFORE YOU LOOK

The first step in recruiting and selecting sales talent is to know what it is you are looking for before you go looking. Amazingly, most companies do less analysis on what they are looking for when filling sales positions than when they are forming the company softball team.

The best way to systematically determine the talents and skills required to excel in your sale, is to examine the qualities of your best performers. If we were to do it for you, we would call it an *Exemplary Performer Analysis*. Simply put, this type of study determines common traits of top performers, which then serve as a guide for the talent search.

Please list below the characteristics of top-performing salespeople in your organization:

1. _____
2. _____
3. _____
4. _____
5. _____
6. _____
7. _____
8. _____
9. _____
10. _____

The exercise that follows lays the groundwork for you to do your own *Exemplary Performer Analysis*. We recommend that you have others involved in your selection process do it along with you and then compare results.

We'll even make the wager[1] that, if you do this as a team:

1. No single characteristic will be on every list
2. No two lists will be the same.

Now, take the list or lists and break down the traits as to whether they are *talents* or *skills* in the following table. Remember that a *talent* is defined as a natural ability, while a *skill* is one that can be taught and learned. If multiple people are doing the exercise, you should group the responses into similar categories. For example, traits like *drive* and *tenacity* could be grouped together.

Talents: Natural Abilities	Skills: Learned Abilities

Informed by this analysis, you have taken the first step toward moving beyond the hapless *I know it when I see it* method and adopting a systematic approach for recruiting and selecting sales talent. Working with a selection team, you have an excellent starting point for a dialogue to achieving consensus on *what you are looking for before you start to look*.

WHAT OUR RESEARCH SHOWS

Table 13.1 represents an amalgam of exemplary performer research we have conducted. It is not necessary that your list resemble this one because every sales process has some unique characteristics. For example, we have a client whose selling process is conducted exclusively with a small number of current clients. There is no prospecting for new clients. Conversely, for another client, the chief success characteristic in their process has to do with prospecting for and finding new clients.

Note: Criteria for recruiting are derived from the talent column, while the training agenda is determined by the skills column.

TALENT OR SKILL?

Please note that a good case could be made for some of the characteristics being on the other list. For example, some would argue that being self-managed is a learned ability. Others would contend that you can teach listening until you are blue in the face, but some people will never get it. Therefore, they would put listening on the talent side of the ledger.

The pertinent point here is that you have the discussion. Hear everyone's views and, if you can't decide, put the trait on both lists. Then, do your best

Table 13.1. Representative sales talents versus sales skills.

Talents: Natural Abilities	*Skills: Learned Abilities*
Motivated	Asks good questions
Remains optimistic	Listening
Creative at finding solutions	Customizes communication
Self-managed	Prospecting
Coachable	Product knowledge
Team player	Presentation skills
Integrity	Consultative selling
Intelligent	Account planning
Maturity	Manage an executive dialogue
Recruitment Criteria	**Training Agenda**

to recruit people who you think have the trait naturally and do your best to teach it, as well. After all, academics have been arguing for nearly a century over what constitutes intelligence and how much of it is native and how much is learned. Once you have determined the requisite talents to succeed in your sales system, there are two methods to objectively measure them:

1. Standardized assessments
2. Behavioral interviews

STANDARDIZED ASSESSMENTS

There's quite an industry out there for standardized testing in selecting sales talent. Most organizations are frustrated by what they consider lackluster sales performance and see a test as a silver bullet solution. If you are not careful, however, you could shoot yourself in the corporate foot. Tests need to satisfy certain technical standards for validity and reliability.

If you are using a test for selection purposes, you should become familiar with the *Uniform Guidelines for Employee Selection Procedures* (Federal Register 1978). It was developed jointly by the friendly folks at the Departments of Justice and Labor, the Civil Service Commission and the Equal Opportunity Commission.

Fundamentally, you will need to ensure that the instrument is valid and that it does not exert an adverse impact on women and minorities. This kind of validity is the predictive variety, which can only be reported in empirical terms. The following are not acceptable as validity indicators:

> . . . all forms of promotional literature; data bearing on the frequency of a procedure's usage; testimonial statements and credentials of sellers, users, or consultants; and other non-empirical or anecdotal accounts of selection practices or selection outcomes. (*Uniform Guidelines for Employee Selection Procedures*)

The best practice in choosing a test is to complete the exercise prescribed earlier in this chapter to ensure that you know what are looking for before you go looking. What is it that sets apart your top performers from the typical ones? What is it that distinguishes salespeople who persist from those who jump ship after three months?

Once you have whittled down your list of traits, do a search of the thousands of instruments out there to identify the ones that best measure traits that define performance in *your* sale. The venerable *Mental Measurements Yearbook* (Pale, et al. 2003) is a good source for finding a test. For example, if *tenacity* and *persistence* are must have qualities for top performers, find instruments that measure those constructs. Don't get caught up in marketing hype or choose a test that assesses *agreeableness,* which may be nice in customer service but not central to sales success.

If all of this sounds daunting, there are consultants (like us) and other professionals who can assist. The investment will prove well worth it with a team possessing the requisite talents to be high performers. Anything less is equivalent to sacrificing a virgin or doing a rain dance.

BEHAVIORAL INTERVIEWS

There's a famous quote attributable to Edward Thorndike, considered the father of psychological testing, that goes, "If it exists, you can measure it." When we cited Thorndike to one of our mentors, Professor Ron Cherry of Juniata College, he responded,: "Yes, but if you can measure it, it probably doesn't matter."

What Ron meant, of course, was that if we restricted ourselves to established measurements, we would have a very limited number of traits we would assess. Let's say that you have determined your top performers have a quality of being able to quickly adapt to different kinds of customers and manage more than one dialogue at the same time. We promise you that the most exhaustive search of the voluminous *Fifteenth Mental Measurements Yearbook (2003)* would not turn up standardized measures of *adapt on the spot* and *manage multiple dialogues during a sales call.*

For these kinds of traits, those that are important but have no corresponding test, the behavioral interview is the best course to pursue. The scope of this chapter does not permit a full treatment of behavioral interviews[2].

Suffice it to say, that as much as possible, behavioral interviews seek to control the subjectivity of typical "What would you do if . . . " kinds of questions by focusing on specific historical behaviors. Rather than allowing the candidate to speculate, behavioral interview questions drill down to specific behaviors and make it harder to fudge a response.

Here are a few examples:

- Describe an accomplishment that took a lot of motivation and self-discipline to complete.
  - Be specific
  - What kept you going?
  - How did you go about it?
- We all regret starting something and not finishing it. What is that something for you?

- Be specific
- What caused you not to complete it?
- What is the most challenging sale you have ever won?
  - Be specific
  - What made it difficult?
  - How long did it take?
  - Any specific strategy or tactic that worked?
  - What kept you going?
  - What was the impact on your next call?
- Everybody in sales deals with rejection and rude behavior. Can you tell me about some you have dealt with recently?
  - Be specific
  - What were you thinking?
  - What did you do next?
- Did you ever lose a big account?
  - Be specific
  - How did you tell your boss?
  - How did you recover?
  - How long did it take?
  - What kept you going?
- Tell me about the last time you surpassed job expectations by going the extra mile.
  - Be specific
  - How long did it take?
  - Any specific strategy or tactic that worked?
  - What kept you going?
- We have all failed to meet a sales goal at one time or another. When was the last time it happened to you?
  - Be specific
  - How did you handle it?
  - How did your boss react?
- What was your calendar like last week?
  - Was it a representative week?
  - How do you plan?
  - How many calls did you make last week? Representative?

RETENTION BEGINS WITH SELECTION

Sales force attrition is a hidden cost borne by most companies that goes well beyond the HR costs of advertising, recruiting, and training. One estimate

(Bliss) is that the costs associated with turnover in a sales position are higher than 250 percent of the annual compensation for that post. Even worse are the disruptions in client relationships and resulting loss in business when new sales faces are rotated in and out of client offices.

Much of the turnover in sales is attributable to the haphazard manner in which selections are made, which too often focus on industry experience rather than native talent. Salespeople cannot learn a talent like *persistence*. They are either hard-wired with it or not.

Investing in a systematic approach to sales force recruitment that focuses on recruiting for talent and employing selection tools, like standardized tests and behavioral interviews, is the surest way to stem the flow of sales for attrition. It may sound paradoxical, but sales force retention begins with selection.

SCORECARD

1. Have you defined the talents that are necessary to succeed in your sales system?
2. Do you focus on natural talents when recruiting?
3. Do you employ objective measures like standardized assessments or behavioral interview questions in selecting sales talent?
4. Or, do you employ the *I know it when I see it* method for selecting sales talent?

NOTES

1 E-mail me at ajtilden@tildensst.com if you are interested in a wager.

2. There is a useful treatment of behavioral interviews by Hoevemeyer, V., *High Impact Interview Questions*, AMACOM, New York, 2005.

Chapter Fourteen

The Recruiting Pipeline

One of the best practices we have identified in recruiting sales talent is to maintain a *recruiting pipeline*. The dynamics of this process are very similar to a sales pipeline with natural stages, or milestones through which sales talent will flow.

Even when we have a contented high performer on our team, we should not fall prey to the trap of thinking she will stay with us in that position forever. In today's economy, we should assume that workers will move through six or more work roles. A talented salesperson may get tapped for a management position, be wooed by the competition, relocate because of a spouse, decide to become Mr. Mom, or even get old and retire.

Further, we want to avoid starting from scratch when we have a key opening, especially in sales where competitors will rush into an unattended territory like sharks sensing blood. Stand-alone media advertising is rarely an efficient or effective way of recruiting sales talent. With a *recruiting pipeline* in place, we have a pre-screened list of prospects we can call and invite to interview. As you will see, our best recruiters in the pipeline system work for free. They are the alumni of our sales program.

MILESTONES TO A RECRUITING PIPELINE

A representative recruiting pipeline is illustrated in figure 14.1 with eight milestones moving from left to right:

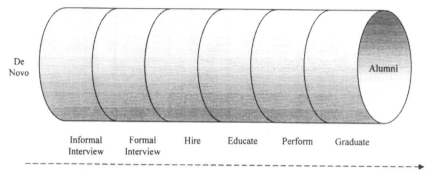

Figure 14.1.   The Recruiting Pipeline.

De Novo

This milestone represents the initial contact with prospective sales talent. Good sales leaders are always prospecting for talent just as good salespeople are always prospecting for new business.

There is no one right way to prospect. But, here are some places to look for De Novo candidates you may want to consider for the next milestone, the *informal interview*:

- Internal technical talent
- Capable salespeople who have made a call on you
- College placement offices
- The competition
- Educators (typically good communicators)
- Salespeople from other industries
- Alumni of your sales program.

The Informal Interview

Once you have done some preliminary screening, extend an invitation to an informal interview. Since *informal* is the operative word here, we recommend that this be done off-site, over lunch, or at places like the gym or golf course.

What you are seeking at this milestone are broad categories of information that can be garnered with questions like:

- Where's home?
- Do you like it here in Moosejaw?
- Where did you go to school?

- Major field? Extracurricular activities?
- How did you get into selling?
- What kinds of accounts do you manage now?
- Do you like selling?
- What do you find to be the biggest challenges?
- What works for you?

If you think the candidate has potential, indicate that you are always interested in sales talent, and ask if he or she would mind a call if an opening came up.

Formal Interview

Inevitably, the opening occurs. Rather than just running a first time advertisement, you should have a Rolodex or electronic bank of potential candidates.

The formal interview is where you drill down in a systematic fashion to assess the native talents of the candidate and how they line up with what you need. This is the step where you employ behavioral interview techniques and or standardized assessments treated in the previous chapter.

The Hire

When your systematic approach to selection indicates someone possesses the talents to succeed, hire them. But don't neglect those you don't select. You owe them a personal follow-up thanking them and assuring them that they have good talents and skills that simply were not the best match for your immediate needs.

Education

Remember the mantra: *Recruit for talent. Train for skills.* While the emphasis with the recruiting pipeline is on recruiting, once talent is selected, don't succumb to the rainmaker myth and think you automatically have a high-performer. There are still skills to be taught and learned to which the upcoming chapter is dedicated.

Performers

This is the stage where you reap the fruits of your recruiting pipeline labor. However, this does not last forever. Like the euphoria that accompanies a big

De Novo	Informal Interview	Formal Interview	Hire	Educate	Perform

Figure 14.2. The Recruiting Pipeline Worksheet

sales win, it is only temporary. And, like top sales performers, exemplary sales recruiters know the best time to return to the beginning of the pipeline is when it appears that everything is going well. Eventually, top sales performers, just like star students, will graduate.

Graduation

When a top sales performer is ready to leave, don't gripe about the loss. Rather, treat the occasion like a graduation. Celebrate. Take them out to dinner and recognize their accomplishments along with their peers and family. Honor them with a gift that broadly displays the company logo.

Alumni

Happy alumni can be your best source for loading the front of the pipeline. Not only will they keep an eye open for sales talent, they will make an enthusiastic referral to your firm as a great place to work. Your investment will be paid back many times over.

RECRUITING PIPELINE WORKSHEET

Turn to the worksheet illustrated in figure 14.2 and begin by estimating the proportion of current performers you anticipate losing in the next year. Use your past experience as a guide. Now start at the beginning of the pipeline and start listing De Novos you intend to contact.

SCORECARD

1. Do you wait for a vacancy to occur on your sales team before you begin recruiting new sales talent?
2. Do you stay in touch with *graduates* of your sales team and seek sales talent referrals from them?
3. When someone leaves your sales team for a better opportunity, do you celebrate their contributions to your team and invite then to join your *alumni association*?

Chapter Fifteen

Train for Skills

Based on the previous two chapters, you have now identified the natural talents requisite to excel in your sales system and differentiated them from skills that can be taught and learned. You have abandoned the *I know it when I see it* method of selection and replaced it with more objective means like behavioral interviews and or standardized tests. Recognizing that attrition among top sales performers is not uncommon, you have a *recruiting pipeline* in place to move quickly when the inevitable opening occurs.

But before we take on the main topic of this chapter, training for skills, there is one more step: assessing the talent level of the *existing* sales team. This is essential because if poor performance is a function of a talent deficiency, no amount of training or coaching for skills will compensate for it. It would be like putting a team of short, slow-footed basketball players through an extensive training regimen on dribbling and shooting. At the end, you would still have short, slow-footed players.

One of the key findings from the exhaustive research upon which *First Break All the Rules* (Buckingham & Coffman 1999) is based is that when it comes to a talent deficit, people cannot and do not change. It is as futile as asking short basketball players to grow taller. The great managers in the *First Break All the Rules* study knew that intuitively. However, the theme of this book is about replacing intuition and gut instincts with a more rational method. We offer one below for evaluating existing team members: the Talents X Skills Matrix™ . This exercise is designed to identify members of the sales team for whom training would be a wasted investment.

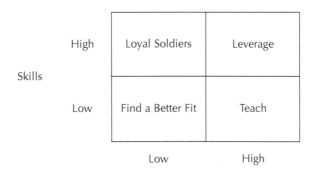

Table 15.1.   The Talents X Skills Matrix™

TALENTS X SKILLS MATRIX™

Once again, talents are natural and god-given. You either have them or you don't. Conversely, skills can be taught and learned. Presupposing that you did the exercise in *Chapter Thirteen: Recruit for Talents and Train for Skills* and have a good sense of which desirable traits are talents and which are skills, your existing team can be plotted in the Talents X Skills Matrix illustrated in table 15.1.

The prescription for managing salespeople who fall into each quadrant is offered below.

Find a Better Fit (Low Talents / Low Skill)

A key lesson from *First Break All the Rules (1999)* research is that you are not doing anyone a favor by retaining team members who lack both skills and talents. The right management solution is to help people in this quadrant find a position that is a better fit. Recognizing that any separation can be time consuming and needs to be executed with care, our prescription is to spend as little time and as few resources as possible on team members who fall in this quadrant. That is what the great managers do.

Loyal Soldiers (Low Talents / High Skills)

This is perhaps the most challenging quadrant to manage. It is likely populated by hardworking *Loyal Soldiers*. Often, they have been around for a long time and are well liked. Basically, there are two options in this quadrant: 1. Accept poor to moderate performance, which is the best they can offer; or 2. Guide them into a position that is a better fit. Our prescription is to do the latter.

Teach (High Talents / Low Skills)

For team members who have native talents but lack the skills requisite for high performance, the management prescription is to teach and coach them. Invest time and resources here because with a proper mix of training and coaching, they will move into the next quadrant (*High Talents / High Skills*) and become high performers.

Leverage (High Talents / High Skills)

The team members who fall in this quadrant are the true stars of our teams. The management trap we want to avoid is ignoring them while we focus on team members who fall in the first two quadrants and lack the talents they will never be able to learn. Instead, we should lavish our highly talented and highly skilled team members with resources and leverage their performance. If they have a weakness or two, rather than harping on it, manage around it and allow them to do what they do best: sell.

The prescriptions offered above may sound harsh for staff falling in the *Find the Better Fit* and the *Loyal Soldier* quadrants. Our experience, however, consistently shows it is right for both the manager *and* the salesperson who is guided to a better fitting position. This has been true for both our personal management experiences, as well as for our clients. We all have talents. But not all of us have the same talents, nor do we all have talent for sales. The sooner we help people find positions where they can express their natural gifts, the more fulfilling it will be for them and the better positioned we are to have a high-performing sales team.

WHERE DO YOU INVEST YOUR TIME?

The well-known *80-20* rule can be traced back to Italian economist Vifredo Pareto, who observed that twenty percent of the people owned eighty percent of the wealth (Cirillo 1978). Since then, it has been invoked to explain many economic and sociological phenomena.

The Talents X Skills Matrix invites us to evaluate how we are investing our management resources. If Pareto's principle applies, sales leaders will find themselves spending eighty percent of their time with salespeople who have talent deficiencies and just twenty percent with the talented team members they should be teaching, coaching, and leveraging.

How about you? Once you have executed the management prescriptions imbedded in the Talent X Skills Matrix, you should flip flop the Pareto proportions and start investing time and resources where it will make a difference. Spend eighty, not twenty, percent of your resources on team members who have the talents to be top performers.

SKILLS FOLLOW THE PROCESS

The first step in planning a sales training curriculum is to have a clear understanding of the nature of the underlying sales process. This should be the product of the work done in *Chapter Ten: Process Driven Selling* where milestones defining important and measurable steps form a pipeline as illustrated in figure 10.1.

Figure 15.1 brings forward that same hypothetical consultative selling pipeline with the skills necessary to succeed in that process added in brackets. Sales leaders for this business would need to take care to teach and coach for *all* of the skill sets listed.

While figure 15.1 is representative, real sales processes are unique to each business. For example, we have a well-established client with very few potential prospects. They are already known by all of them, and prospecting skills like developing referral resources are irrelevant. On the other hand, we have yet another client, relatively new in their marketplace, for whom prospecting skills are the most vital to their success.

The pertinent point is to know your *own* process and the distinctive skills necessary to advance from one milestone to the next. Don't take the training approach of pulling the team in every so often and throwing some training at them in the hope that some of it will stick. This is the equivalent of periodically sacrificing a virgin and not really being sure why.

SKILLS NOT MOTIVATIONAL SPEAKERS

It is beyond the scope of this book to provide training materials for all of the skill sets listed in figure 15.1 Instead, we critique what we consider to be four helpful sales skills resources that transcend most sales skills processes. First, however, it is important to clarify that we are addressing sales *skills* and not sales *motivation* events or materials. It is an important distinction to keep in mind, especially if you are contemplating bringing in a high power motivational

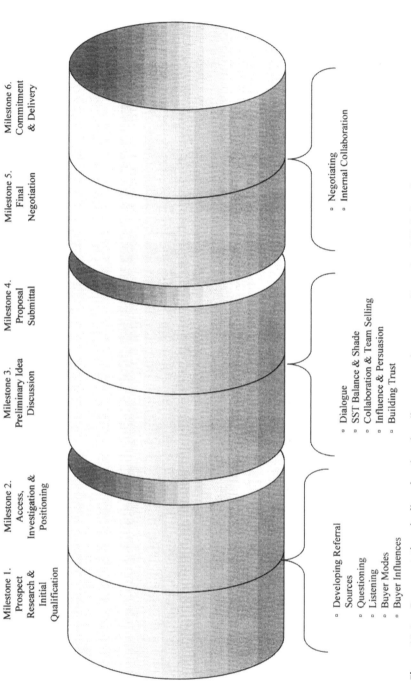

Figure 15.1. Representative pipeline showing six milestones and corresponding sales skills in brackets.

Milestone 1.
Prospect
Research &
Initial
Qualification

Milestone 2.
Access,
Investigation &
Positioning

Milestone 3.
Preliminary Idea
Discussion

Milestone 4.
Proposal
Submittal

Milestone 5.
Final
Negotiation

Milestone 6.
Commitment
& Delivery

- Developing Referral
  Sources
- Questioning
- Listening
- Buyer Modes
- Buyer Influences

- Dialogue
- SST Balance & Shade
- Collaboration & Team Selling
- Influence & Persuasion
- Building Trust

- Negotiating
- Internal Collaboration

speaker to jumpstart sales, as the fictional Mitch & Murray did in *Glengarry GlenRoss,* when they brought in Blake ("I made $950,000 last year. How much did you make?") to rally the troops.

Back in Chapter Seven we described that opening scene when Blake announces a third prize has been added to the monthly sales contest: *"You're fired!"* Many organizations invest in outside motivational speakers, like Blake, hoping that incentives like a new car, a set of steak knives, or the threat of being fired will result in a positive spike in performance. In fact, there's a cottage industry of motivational speakers like Lou Holtz, reminiscing about Notre Dame football heroics, and Tony Robbins, inspiring people to walk on hot coals. Sometimes inspirational films are used instead of speakers. In an effort to create a "business culture focused on selling" managers of Sears are required to watch the film *Miracle on Ice* about the 1980 gold medal U.S. hockey team. The hope is that this event will inspire better customer service (*New York Times*, April 13, 2006).

That is not what we are talking about here. It is not that motivation is unimportant. Clearly it is. However, long-term, positive motivation does not come from motivational speakers. Rather, it is derived from well thought out structures that reward the right kinds of behaviors plus leadership that provides intrinsic rewards customized to each member of the sales team. This combination puts even highly ambitious sales production goals within everyone's reach.

SALES PERFORMANCE FORMULA

The best way to illustrate the relationship between *skills* and *motivation* is with the following formula:

$$Sales\ Performance = Ability\ x\ Motivation$$

Ability: Talents & Skills

Ability is a mix of talents and skills. The former are accidents of birth, while the latter can be taught and learned. As the formula suggests, being both talented and skilled is not enough, one must be motivated as well. Indeed, being multiplicative in character, the sales performance formula prescribes that ability (the combination of talents and skills) coupled with zero motivation will produce zero performance.

Motivation: Extrinsic & Intrinsic Rewards

The difference between the two kinds of rewards has been treated in *Chapter Eleven: Formal Structure*. Basically, the former are external to the salesperson and typically come in the form of salaries and bonuses. Conversely, the latter, while just as powerful, come from within the salesperson. They have to do with emotions, like sense of achievement, recognition, and the quality of interpersonal relationships formed with both co-workers and leaders. Our experience with one-off motivational speakers, even famous ones, is that they are just that: one-off.

In summary, we are not disputing the importance of motivation. Rather, we are making the case that motivation is, in fact, *too important* to be left to a rah-rah rally led by a Richard Simmons running around in his shorts or even a General Norman Schwarzkopf marching around in his uniform. Serious treatment of rewards requires attention to the structure as treated in Chapter Eleven and leaders who are capable of building meaningful relationships with their team members, ones that they find intrinsically rewarding.

ANNOTATION OF SALES SKILLS RESOURCES

While sales skills follow the unique process of an organization, there are fundamentally four models that offer generic value across almost all consultative sales processes. They are also anchored in respectable research and theory and thereby consistent with the core theme of this book, which emphasizes reason and science over mythology and motivational speakers.

1. Rackham's (1988) *SPIN Selling:* a model for questioning
2. PfP Consulting's *Know What, How & Why*[1]
3. Miller & Heiman's (1998) *The New Strategic Selling:* multiple decision influences
4. Tilden's (2000) *SST®: Successful Selling to Type:* customizing communication to different personality types.

SPIN Selling

As noted previously (*Chapter Three: Closers*), prior to Rackham's study, the best companies in the world were pursuing the closing myth. However, Rackham's team discovered just the opposite: the key to winning major and complex sales was not *closing*, but *opening* the sale with good questions.

Based on his research, Rackham developed a questioning model that goes by the acronym SPIN with each letter representing a category of question: *S (Situations); P (Problem); I(Implication); and N (Need pay–off).*

A favorite question of ours is to ask training classes why it is that Rackham's research highlighted questioning and not listening? Perhaps it is a more fitting question for a research methods class than it is for one on consultative selling. But, the answer is that a researcher sitting in and observing one of the sales calls in Rackham's study could *hear*, even record and later classify, questions that were asked during the interview. However, the equally important investigation skill of listening was indiscernible to the senses of that same researcher.

In our own training we place an equal emphasis on both questioning and listening. Be wary of the hazard of recently trained and well-intended salespeople placing so much emphasis on the quality and category of the question that they forget to listen. A good question planned and asked, not followed by empathic listening, is a wasted exercise.

Know What, How, and Why Questioning Model

Successful consultative salespeople build trust-based relationships with their clients on solid platforms of *dialogue*. In their investigation efforts, they seek to understand a client's business at three levels, which we refer to in shorthand as *Know What, How, and Why*.

- Know What – This focuses the salesperson on understanding *what* the client is trying to achieve, not in any single transaction or purchase decision, but in strategic performance terms as a business. Examples of performance goals include increasing market share in key product lines, overall growth in sales and profitability, and achieving target levels of performance in areas such as return on capital, earnings per share, and shareholder value. Performance goals, which can exist at both the enterprise and strategic business unit levels, thus reflect a company's strategic scorekeeping system.
  - The primary objective of a consultative salesperson is to position himself as a performance resource in the eyes of the client. This requires getting access to, and building dialogue with, the performance thinkers and decision makers in the client organization. After all, we all recognize that, in large organizations with elaborate decision-making hierarchies, there will be some decision makers who are primarily *performance* thinkers and others who are primarily *execution* thinkers.
- Know How – This focuses the salesperson on understanding *how* the client is currently seeking to reach its strategic performance goals. Conversations about specific client needs take place at the level of Know How. Most salespeople never venture beyond this level in their conversations with clients, which is fine if all they hope to accomplish is making transactional sales.
- Know Why - Consultative salespeople recognize the importance of understanding the *context* of client needs, and that is defined by *Know What*. It is

this context knowledge that enables a consultative salesperson to apply greater creativity to ideas and solutions. The combination of Know What and Know How knowledge thus provides a salesperson with true insight into the client's thinking and decision-making. This is the essence of Know Why – the rationale behind Know What and Know How. Salespeople with Know Why understanding are thus able to exert much more influence over their clients because they understand the genealogy of the client's needs. A salesperson who identifies a client *need*, but who cannot trace that need back to one or more of the client's performance goals, does not really understand the client and will be at a competitive disadvantage with a salesperson who has had the patience and discipline to conduct a more thorough investigation of the client.

In summary, there are two kinds of conversation a salesperson can have with a client. *Execution* conversations take place in the realm of Know How and focus on immediate client needs. Typical sales performers operate here. *Performance* conversations, on the other hand, take place in the realm of Know What and focus on the goals that are most important to the client. Thus, client needs can only be truly understood within the context of the performance goals from which they have arisen. Exemplary sales performers build dialogue at both execution and performance levels in a client organization.

Finally, a salesperson's investigation should also be guided by seeking to understand the client's business *holistically*. Think of this as following the client's production chain and *seeing through to the other side of their business*. Salespeople with *holistic knowledge* can answer the following types of questions about their best clients.

- What are the client's key lines of business?
- What strategies is the client pursuing in an effort to create and sustain competitive advantage?
- What is the profile of the client's ideal customer relationship?
- How does the client win new customers? How do they keep customers? How do they lose customers?

In a recent workshop we conducted for a major European bank, a foreign exchange salesperson described how his holistic knowledge of a client in the fashion business had enabled him to differentiate himself from other salespeople and dramatically increase the volume and profitability of the business he was doing with the client. The fashion designer's key customers are large department stores and up-market retail menswear chains. As the salesperson described it, the buyers in the department stores and retail chains are very powerful, creating a true buyer's market. In order to be competitive, the salesperson's client had to offer fixed prices on its fashion line an entire season in advance. Thus, in February the designer's salespeople would be pitching the upcoming fall fashion line with fixed prices (fully six months before the orders would be filled). With this holistic understanding, the salesperson was able to gain insights into the client's currency risk management strategy that other salespeople didn't have (because they weren't asking the right kinds of questions). Thus, when the salesperson called the client's Chief Financial Officer (CFO) with an idea, he was able to frame it up by saying, "We've got an idea that we believe will help make your salespeople more competitive. Can we come and talk to you about it?" That sounds a lot different than salespeople at other banks who would call to say, "We can offer a good deal on a financial product today." The CFO certainly thought it did.

A salesperson cannot be truly consultative without exercising the twin investigative skills of questioning and listening. Using the performance approach to questioning and listening and developing holistic knowledge of your client's business should be core modules in any consultative selling curriculum.

Multiple Decision Influences

One of the major differentiators between transactional and consultative selling is the presence of multiple buying influences at the consultative level. When selling a commodity, the seller typically seeks to influence one buyer that his or her product is the best value and that it is easy to acquire. As noted previously, transactional selling relies purely on execution conversations and emphasizes working hard and getting in front of as many qualified decision makers as possible. The prescription is to knock on the door, make the pitch, ask for the order, and move on to the next door as quickly as possible.

At the consultative level, however, there is more than one buying influence at play. And, while working hard never hurts, it is not enough unless accompanied by smart strategies for various buyer influences. Miller and Heiman's *Strategic Selling* (1985) and *New Strategic Selling* (1998) make major contributions in understanding the multiple buyer influences at play.

In major and complex sales, there are four influences that you need to manage: e*conomic* (Top of the food chain; usually performance thinkers; and can say "yes"); *user* (More than one person who will be using your solution on a regular basis); *technical* (Interested in technical specifications and can't say "yes" but can say "no") and advocate or coach (the inside source who can explain who play s the aforementioned roles).

The Miller & Heiman decision influences model is easy to master and indispensable to building a winning profile for consultative selling. As we often say during training, "If your competitor has a strategy for, and is building relationships with, all four influences, and you are only focusing on one or two, we don't like your chances."

SST®: Successful Selling to Type

While the previous three models help salespeople *understand* and profile their clients, Tilden's (2000) SST® provides a method for packaging communication when it is the salesperson's turn to be *understood*. The core premise of SST® is that it is a human tendency to send messages to others the way *we*, but not necessarily *they*, would like to receive them. Anchored in Jung's theory of personality types, familiar to many through the Myers Briggs Type Indicator (MBTI), SST® emphasizes the principles of *balance* and *shade*. The former is employed when selling to buying committees or when it is not possible to determine the communication preferences of the buyer(s). The seller then takes care to ensure that messages are *balanced* to appeal to all communication preferences. However, when the seller is able to read behavioral cues of the buyer well enough to be confident of his or her communication preferences, messages are *shaded* in that direction. For example, Sensors are given a lot of facts and details up front, while big picture implications are filled in later on. Conversely, presentations to Intuitive-preferred clients lead with the big picture, while exercising care to keep facts concise.

To use SST effectively it is not necessary to master all of the sixteen personality types in the MBTI model. Instead, the salesperson only needs to know one well: his own.

SCORECARD

1. Have you completed the Talents X Skills Matrix for your sales team?
2. Do you invest most of your time with talented members of the sales team?
3. Does your sales training curriculum match your underlying sales process?
4. Are you or your salespeople versatile enough to engage clients in both performance and execution conversation?
5. Do you differentiate between sales motivation speakers and sales skills trainers?

NOTE

1. The source of the Know What, How & Why questioning model is unpublished training materials authored by Harry Koolen, managing partner of PfP Consulting, Inc. (tildensst.com)

THE NEW MYTH & PLAN OF ACTION

"I hear and I forget. I see and I remember. I do and I understand."

Confucius

Chapter Sixteen

The New Myth: Automation

A new sales myth has emerged. Businesses are investing billions in it. Yet estimates by a well-regarded research organization (Gartner Group) are that most of those efforts have failed to deliver results (Rigby 2002). This modern day snake dance is joined by priests with titles like Chief Information Officer. It goes by the acronym CRM (Customer Relationship Management) or its cousin SFA (Sales Force Automation).

CRM has gone from buzzword to bad word (Bach 2002). The first wave of CRM/SFA installations in the 1990s failed to deliver on the promise of dramatically increasing enterprise sales and profitability. One industry commentator cited in London's *Financial Times* (August 24, 2000) estimated that fully eighty percent of CRM projects met neither the requirements of the user sales forces nor the strategic requirements of the organization.

This chapter is not intended to be a buyers' guide to CRM/SFA systems. Instead, we want to address one of the most common reasons why much of the investment that businesses have made in CRM/SFA systems over the past fifteen years has not produced the hoped-for benefits: the failure to define a sales process *before* installing sales automation. Once again, the system, not automation, is the solution.

While many of the lessons learned during the failed first wave of CRM/SFA are producing smarter IT investment decisions today, we continue to be surprised at how often we encounter organizations that have committed to multi-million dollar sales technology installations without first having developed a sales process.

WHY A SALES PROCESS BEFORE AUTOMATION

Many salespeople (and even some sales managers) resist the notion of defining a sales process. This is especially true for consultative sales where many believe instead that every sale is unique. Like their Paleolithic ancestors, they would prefer to pray to the gods before every hunt, rather than follow a step-by-step process. We would not dispute the notion of the unique characteristics of each sale, at the margin. After all, each one involves different people and, often, distinctive solutions to special problems. However, even across multiple product categories, consultative sales do (and should) follow an underlying pattern.

There are many reasons for defining your sales process, not all of which are necessarily related to the eventual purchase and installation of a CRM/ SFA system.

Improve the Thoroughness and Quality of Effort

While there is nothing necessarily wrong with looking for opportunities to accelerate the sales process, sloppiness and poor follow-up will undermine a sales effort very quickly. Having a rigorous sales process model builds personal discipline and good pipeline management habits.

Improve the Consistency of Effort

A well-designed sales process helps salespeople understand what needs to get done, and knowing what to do leads to more consistent effort and performance. This is especially important when selling products or services with long lead times, where sustained effort across an entire pipeline of leads is vital.

Introduce Efficiencies into the Business Development Process

Every salesperson is faced with making decisions each day related to how they will spend their time. These decisions usually involve trade-offs between higher value and lower value sales-related activities. Higher value activities can include writing proposals, booking sales calls and presentations, or doing certain types of research in support of upcoming calls. Lower value activities typically include things like updating activity reports and databases or completing expense statements. When faced with the necessity of completing both types of tasks, a well-designed sales process can help the salesperson use his or her time much more efficiently and make smarter trade-off decisions.

Facilitate Delegation and Ultimately Automation

Even consultative selling can involve repetitive tasks. With a sales process in place, these tasks can be more easily delegated, freeing the salesperson to focus on the more discrete, often more labor intensive, higher value tasks.

There's Nothing to Automate

Finally, without a sales process in place, there is nothing to automate, except one of the sales myths: Rainmakers, Closers, Schmooze, or Field of Dreams.

COMPUTERS CAN'T BUILD RELATIONSHIPS

The subtle interplay of rational and relationship decision factors that characterizes consultative buying decisions really lies at the heart of the consultative sales process (see table 10.1 in Chapter Ten). This also underscores the importance of the early investigation and positioning stages of the process. Pre-defined sales process and pipeline management modules in CRM/SFA software systems rarely capture these important nuances. They should be designed into the CRM/SFA relevant modules only *after* a customer acquisition and retention strategy and its supporting sales process have been determined (Rigby 2002, 103). As James Rager, vice chairman of Royal Bank of Canada, pointed out, ". . . the idea of CRM as a self-contained solution is dead. Rather, it's got to be something that supplements your overall approach to your business . . ." (Bach 2002).

Many organizations learned these lessons the hard way during the first cycle of CRM/SFA. Instead of defining their customer strategies and sale processes before making CRM/SFA purchases, they did it after the fact and found themselves having to work with (or around) the pre-defined modules that came bundled in the software packages. What they quickly learned was that, if the sales process and pipeline management modules in your CRM/SFA system are not an accurate reflection of the milestones in your underlying sales process, you quickly forfeit all of the benefits of having a well thought out customer strategy and sales process already in place. Salespeople and sales managers ended up having to force fit sales process activity data into sales milestone categories in the CRM/SFA that bore little resemblance to the underlying realities of how salespeople advanced through the process, one milestone at a time.

GARBAGE IN – GARBAGE OUT (GIGO)

Not surprisingly, getting automation ahead of real process and practice led to another problem that undermined the CRM/SFA investment: salespeople either stopped using the CRM/SFA system or put garbage in it. Even today, with all the sales automation mistakes of the recent past in full view for businesses to learn from, one of the biggest challenges facing organizational leadership remains getting salespeople to use the CRM/SFA system. When that system is not designed around the customer strategy and sales process, it just gives salespeople another excuse to avoid using it. Even if salespeople can be compelled to use a poorly designed system, the data that sales managers draw from the system will be of little practical use for coaching and process monitoring if the sales team entered garbage data. As the old GIGO axiom goes: garbage in—garbage out.

Worse yet, automating a flawed or ill-defined sales process can lead to a system that actually exaggerates the flaws. Recall from Chapter Eight what Lou Gerstner found at IBM, "People don't do what you expect but what you inspect." (2002, 211). It is just human nature that sales scorekeeping systems drive the behavior of salespeople. If you count it, they will do it, whether *it* makes sense or not.

Whether you are a salesperson or a sales manager, you must understand how your sales process works and how your clients make complex purchase decisions *before* you can harness technology to improve sales performance. Otherwise, too much of the sales effort can be misdirected, wasting both time and opportunity in pursuit of a modern sales myth.

SCORECARD

1. Does your sales process undergird your existing CRM/SFA?
2. If you are planning to invest in CRM/SFA, have you first refined your sales process?
3. If you have CRM/SFA, do your salespeople use it?
4. If you have CRM/SFA, do your salespeople enter good data or garbage?

Chapter Seventeen

Plan of Action

"We may give advice, but we cannot give conduct." Benjamin Franklin

"Education is not the filling of a pail, but the lighting of a fire." W.B. Yeats

"To be effective the knowledge worker is, first of all, expected to get the right things done." Peter Drucker

Whether it be *conduct*, *lighting a fire*, or *getting the right things done*, the greatest value from this book will be derived by the reader who moves beyond sitting back and reading it to making a commitment to specific actions to improve his or her selling or sales management. To frame it in Drucker's (2001, 191-206) terminology, the preceding chapters should help the reader decide what the *right things* are. This concluding chapter offers guidance in determining specific plans of action for *doing the right things* to improve sales performance.

Some of the right things are universal, while others are determined by the reader's susceptibility to one or more of the four myths. Accordingly, we begin by revisiting the Scorecard questions posed at the conclusions of Chapters Two through Four in the spirit of diagnosing the implications of each myth before prescribing corrective actions.

DO YOU BELIEVE IN RAINMAKERS?

Consider these questions brought forward from Chapter Two to assess the degree to which you are susceptible to the Rainmaker myth.

1. Do you use the term *rainmaker* for top-performing salespeople in your organization?

2. Does your firm hold the view that, *"Well, some of us can do this and some of us can't"?*
3. Do you afford special privileges to those who can *make it rain?*
4. Have you had an executive level conference recently about the need to hire some rainmakers?
5. Is the work of your organization highly technical, performed by licensed or certified professionals?
6. Do the high-performing technical experts harbor a view, private or public, that the work they do is more important than selling?
7. Does your organization aspire to become so well known and respected that, someday, you won't have to rely on rainmakers?
8. Does your organization believe that salespeople are just affable, back slapping guys (generic, of course) who had low GPAs in college and now play a lot of golf?

RAINMAKER CORRECTIVE ACTIONS

If you believe in rainmakers, you likely have some people in the organization trying to grow the business or professional practice to the exclusion of others. Those who are chosen as rainmakers are believed to possess a *sales personality*. Since there is no such thing[1], the two greatest risks related to the Rainmaker myth are: 1. People who could be contributing to the sales effort are not and 2. Those who are anointed rainmaker status are likely relying on some trait like *charisma* instead of following a sales process and acquiring the skills needed to succeed in it. The appropriate corrective actions are to:

1. Examine what it takes to succeed in your underlying sales process. Map out the milestones and assemble them in a pipeline using Chapter Ten as a resource.
2. Determine the abilities to succeed in the sales process. Settle on which abilities are talents and which are skills (Chapter Thirteen).
3. Reevaluate who has been charged with business or practice development responsibilities.
4. Follow the mantra outlined in Chapters Thirteen and Fifteen: *Recruit for talent. Train for skills.*

DO YOU BELIEVE IN CLOSERS?

Consider the following questions brought forward from Chapter Three to determine if you are pursuing the Closer myth.

1. Do you conduct training programs that emphasize closing skills?
2. Do you use the term *close* as a synonym for *win*?
3. In forecasting sales through pipelines or sales funnels, do you put an emphasis on the latter stages of the sales cycle?

CLOSER CORRECTIVE ACTIONS

The Closer myth could be the most hazardous of all because those who subscribe to it could actually be engaging in sales behaviors that discourage, rather than encourage, customers from buying. This is especially true if you are operating in a consultative sales process where the key is *opening* the sale with good questions rather than manipulating a prospect into a close. Do you know anyone who likes to be manipulated? Neither do we.

If you or your sales force are operating under the Closer myth:

1. Determine the mode or modes in which your customers or prospects are buying (transactional, consultative, or enterprise) using Chapter Nine as a resource.
2. If it is a transactional sales process, reliance on the *closing myth* is less of an issue. As noted previously, the success formula in transactional sales relies on the efficiencies of getting in front of as many prospects as possible, letting the product do the talking, and asking for the order.
3. However, if your process is consultative in nature you need to carefully map out the milestones in the process (Chapter Ten) giving meticulous attention to the crucial investigation stage. Closers tend to bypass the early milestones in the consultative sales process and focus prematurely on the latter ones.

DO YOU BELIEVE IN SCHMOOZE?

Consider the following questions brought forward from Chapter Four to determine if you are subscribing to the Schmooze myth:

1. Do you dedicate more than ten percent of your sales budget to entertaining clients and other schmoozing?
2. When you host functions like golf or ski outings, do you refer to them as business or practice development?
3. Do you spend the same or more on schmoozing than you do on training and skill building?

4. Do you have a shared and replicable sales system that outlines significant steps and milestones?
5. Do you monitor pipeline or sales funnel activities to forecast sales?

SCHMOOZE CORRECTIVE ACTIONS

As mentioned in Chapter Four, Schmooze is the most demeaning myth because it implies that clients and customers can be bought. It is also dangerous because it diverts resources from selecting salespeople with talents and training them in sales skills, and instead spends those resources on entertainment. If you or your sales force are operating under the Schmooze myth:

1. Examine the recruiting and selection budget. Is it adequate?
2. Examine the training budget? Is it adequate?
3. If the answer to either or both questions is "no", reallocate resources from the entertainment budget to the deficient recruiting or training budgets.

DO YOU BELIEVE IN FIELD OF DREAMS?

Consider the following questions brought forward from Chapter Five to determine if you are subscribing to the Field of Dreams myth.

1. Is your business development strategy to *out-engineer* the competition?
2. Are salespeople assigned second-class or necessary evil status in the organization?
3. Does your sales training emphasize technical product knowledge over selling skills?
4. Do you neglect to use salespeople as a source of market intelligence?
5. Are your salespeople trained in a replicable sales process with milestones that can be plotted in a pipeline?

FIELD OF DREAMS CORRECTIVE ACTIONS

While closing may be the most dangerous myth and schmooze the most demeaning, Field of Dreams is the most common. This is especially true in organizations where there are technical products or services that have been developed or engineered by staff holding engineering, MBA, or Ph.D. degrees. These organizations also tend to pursue the *inside-out* as contrasted to *out-*

side-in (Chapter Seven) approach to business, believing it is all about them and their products.

It is not. Rather, it is all about the value the product creates for the customer. A talented and skilled sales team is indispensable to uncovering customer needs and determining how and where value can be created for the customer. As Peter Drucker (2005, 187) once observed, ". . . anyone who asks the question, 'What does the customer really buy?' will win the race."

If you or your sales force are operating under the Field of Dreams myth:

1. Examine your strategic planning. If it is indeed *inside-out*, take the necessary steps to adopt an *outside-in* approach to strategic planning that puts customer needs first.
2. Take steps to systematically gather and organize the market trend information the sales force routinely sees and hears in the field. Ask them what they are hearing from their customers.
3. Evaluate the training offered to the sales force to ensure that it addresses both product knowledge and selling skills.

While the prescriptions outlined above are guided by susceptibility of subscribing to one or more of the sales myths, the following three sections present generic actions for all, and are organized around the *Strategy, Structure and People*™ model.

STRATEGY ACTION STEPS

1. If you are an *inside-out* organization, make a commitment to adopt an *outside-in* approach to strategic planning (Chapters Seven and Nine).
2. Ask representative people from the four levels of your organization (directors, CEO, sales managers, and salespeople) if they *know the plan* and are able to list the top three strategic initiatives for the quarter. If the answers you get are varied, it means the strategic plan has not been sufficiently translated throughout the organization. Develop and implement a plan to translate the strategy (Chapters Seven and Eight).
3. Commit to a strategic planning process that models what high-performing organizations do as outlined in Chapter Eight. This means strategic planning that is:
   a. An ongoing process
   b. Summarized in a brief document
   c. Action-oriented
   d. Reviewed regularly

  e. Measurable
  f. Translated throughout the organization
  g. Budget driving
4. Assess how your customers or clients are buying using the Rackham &
   DeVincentis buyer mode model described in Chapter Nine. Segment your
   markets by transactional, consultative, and enterprise buyers.
5. Examine what it takes to succeed in your underlying sales process. Map
   out the milestones and assemble them in a pipeline (Chapter Ten).
6. Once your pipeline is in place, conduct regular (at least weekly) pipeline
   reviews (Chapter Ten).
7. Maintain pipeline balance by conducting weekly 3+3+3 exercises.

STRUCTURE ACTION STEPS

1. Examine your metrics to ensure you are measuring the right things. Take
   special care that you are not using measures suitable for transactional sales
   that require *working hard* for a consultative process that calls for *working
   smart*. If necessary, adjust your metrics using Chapter Eleven as a resource.
2. Make certain you are rewarding the right behaviors. Sales organizations
   tend to emphasize the tangible wins that flow from the end of the pipeline.
   While recognizing and even celebrating important wins is appropriate, be
   mindful of neglecting the early milestones in the pipeline, those that are
   essential to successful and sustained sales performance (Chapters Ten and
   Eleven).
3. Success with major and complex sales often takes many months and sometimes longer. Consider the advancement from one milestone to the next in
   such a process as achieving a *mini-sale* and reward it.
4. Tangible extrinsic rewards, like commissions, work well for the final win,
   but are less effective for the milestones that precede it. Develop and implement a plan to use intrinsic rewards when salespeople achieve early and
   middle pipeline milestones that: a. Fit the culture and b. Are customized to
   the receiver. Chapters Ten and Eleven should serve as helpful resources for
   points two through four.
5. While every sales organization gives painstaking attention to how it provides extrinsic rewards, too often they neglect the flip side: the occasional,
   yet inevitable, need to render consequences. Make a commitment to con-
   front and deliver consequences for undesirable behaviors in a professional
   and timely fashion.
6. Examine your organization chart for telltale horizontal and dotted lines
   (Chapter Twelve). If you have too many, you are in an organization where

excessive energy is being channeled into the informal structure. This serves to undermine the formal structure and the achievement of its goals and objectives. Making the formal and informal structures congruent is always a difficult process and sometimes impossible to achieve in its entirety. Nonetheless, it is an important undertaking. Begin by making a commitment to fill positions based on the abilities (talents and skills) required to excel in each job, and not the informal or political influence people possess.

7. Complete the exercise in table 12.1, which lists the terms of the psychological contract: *If I do this . . . I get that.* Take as much care in managing the terms of the psychological contract as you do with formal contracts.

PEOPLE ACTION STEPS

1. Complete the exercises in Chapter Thirteen to differentiate between the natural talents and learnable skills necessary to succeed in the underlying sales process.

2. Evaluate your selection process. Would you characterize it as, *I know it when I see it?* If the answer is "yes", develop and execute a systematic recruiting and selection process using standardized tests and/or behavioral interviews as tools.

3. Put a *recruiting pipeline* into place. Begin by completing the Recruiting Pipeline Worksheet, figure 14.2.

4. Complete the Talents X Skills Matrix™ in table 15.1. Develop and execute a plan to manage salespeople who fall into each of the quadrants: Find a Better Fit, Loyal Soldiers, Teach, and Leverage.

5. Use the Talents X Skills Matrix™ to assess where you are investing your management time. Have you fallen prey to Pareto's principle, meaning that you are spending most of your time with problem performers in the Find a Better Fit and or Loyal Soldiers quadrants? If you are, redirect your resources to salespeople in the Teach and Leverage quadrants.

6. Figure 15.1 is a representative pipeline showing six milestones with corresponding sales skills. Using figure 15.1 as a resource, plot your pipeline showing the skill sets that correspond to each milestone. Develop and implement a plan to provide training and coaching for those skills.

AUTOMATION ACTION STEPS

1. Implementing CRM or SFA systems before the underlying sales process is in place, only serves to exaggerate existing problems. Further, CRM and

SFA technologies are expensive. If you are planning to automate, be certain that you have addressed the action items listed in this Chapter Seventeen first. You will enjoy a much higher return on investment.

NOTE

1. The sign over the sales manager's door in *Glengarry GlenRoss* has it wrong. Salesmen are made, not born.

References

Anastasi, A. *Psychological Testing.* 5th ed. New York: Macmillan, 1982.

Anderson, J. "Running the Gauntlet at Wal-Mart." *Inc. Magazine,* November 2003: 93-97.

Armstrong, K. *A Short History of Myth.* Edinburgh: Cannongate, 2005.

Bach, D. "Disappointment with CRM Blamed on Lofty Expectations." *American Banker,* March 7, 2002.

Bion, W. *Experience in Groups.* London: Tavistock, 1961.

Bliss, W. "Cost of Employee Turnover." *The Advisor.* www.isquare.com.

Buckingham, M & Coffman, C. *First Break All the Rules.* New York: Simon & Schuster, 1999.

Charan, R. & Tichy, N. *Every Business Is a Growth Business.* New York: Three Rivers Press, 1998.

Cirillo, R. *The Economics of Vilfredo Pareto.* London: Taylor & Francis, 1978.

Conway, N. & Briner, R. *Understanding Psychological Contracts at Work.* Oxford: Oxford University Press, 2005.

Deutsch, C. "Xerox, Fading Copier King, Hasn't Used Its Innovations." *The New York Times,* October 19, 2000.

Drucker, P., *The Essential Drucker*, New York, Collins, 2005.

Federal Register. *Uniform Guidelines on Employee Selection Procedures.* Vol. 43, No. 166 (August 25, 1978): 38296-309.

Financial Times. "Customers Urged to Cutback Before They Buy." *www.ft.com.,* August 24, 2000.

Gerstner, L. *Who Says Elephants Can't Dance?* New York: HarperCollins, 2002.

Godin, Seth. *Permission Marketing.* New York: Simon & Schuster, 1999.

Hammer, M. & Champy, J. *Reengineering the Organization.* New York: HarperCollins, 2003.

Heiman, S. & Sanchez, D. *The New Strategic Selling.* New York: Warner Books, 1998.

Hoevemeyer, V. *High Impact Interview Questions.* New York: AMACOM, 2005.

Kohn, A. *Punished by Rewards* New York: Houghton Mifflin, 1993.

Maraniss, D. W*hen Pride Still Mattered*. New York: Simon & Schuster, 1999.

Miller, R. & Heiman, S. *Strategic Selling*. New York: William Morrow, 1985.

Pale, B., Impera, J, & Spies, R. *The Fifteenth Mental Measurements Yearbook.* Lincoln, Neb.: University of Nebraska Press, 2003.

Peterson, G. *High Impact Sales Force Automation*. Boca Raton, Fl.: CRC Press, 1997.

Rackham, N. *Major Account Sales Strategy.* New York: McGraw-Hill, 1989.

———. *Spin Selling.* New York: McGraw-Hill, 1988.

Rackham, N. & DeVincentis, J. *Rethinking the Sales Force.* New York: McGraw-Hill, 1999.

Rackham, N., Friedman, L. & Ruff, R. *Getting Partnering Right.* New York: McGraw-Hill, 1996.

Rackham, N., Friedman, L. & Ruff, R. *Managing Major Sales.* New York: HarperCollins, 1991.

Rigby, D., Reichheld, F. & Schefter, P. "Avoid the Perils of CRM." *Harvard Business Review.* February 2002: 101-9.

Sawyer, R. *Sun tzu The Art of War*, translated. New York: Barnes & Noble, 1994.

Sullivan, L. *South American Indians*. New York: MacMillan, 1987.

Wilkinson, P. *Illustrated Dictionary of Mythology*. New York: DK Publishing, 1998.

Index

About the Author

Dr. **Arnold Tilden** is the principal of Tilden & Associates and a partner in PfP Consulting, firms that help clients grow their businesses through performance consulting, training, recruitment and selection, strategic planning and executive development. He has served as the lead consultant on performance improvement projects for clients like The Federal Reserve System, Barclays Global Investors, Credit Suisse First Boston, Fortis Bank (Brussels, Amsterdam & Luxembourg), BNP Paribas (Paris, Hong Kong, Bahrain & Mumbai), Johnson Controls, KPMG and Johns Hopkins University. He has also worked with regional Pennsylvania firms like Bink Architectural Partnership, Members 1st Federal Credit Union, McKonly & Asbury CPAs and SPE Federal Credit Union.

Tilden earned his doctorate from Temple University in educational psychology and is a specialist with the Myers Briggs Type Indicator. He has effectively used that model to advance leadership skills, career development and teamwork. He is the founder and author of *Successful Selling to Type: SST®* a sales model which improves communication effectiveness by applying MBTI principles and concepts. Prior to launching his consulting practice, Tilden served as a college dean and taught psychology and management courses.